LEE ROY

MY STORY OF FAITH, FAMILY AND FOOTBALL

By Lee Roy Jordan
With Steve Townsend

LEE ROY
MY STORY OF FAITH, FAMILY AND FOOTBALL

Proceeds from Lee Roy: My Story of Faith, Family and Football will be donated to the Lee Roy Jordan Endowed Academic Scholarship at the University of Alabama and to the Paul W. Bryant Museum.

ISBN: 978-0-9991868-0-0

CONTENTS

The following individuals took time from their schedules to share their memories of Lee Roy Jordan with Steve Townsend, Kim Bryan and Courtney Haden. Each has played a significant role in Lee Roy's life.

ACKNOWLEDGEMENTS

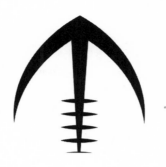

JOE NAMATH FOREWORD

My first impression of Lee Roy Jordan was what I heard Coach Bryant saying to him at practice, and watching him work on the football field. As freshmen, we just tried to lay low with the varsity.

Those guys were the real studs and leaders. Some of the varsity players were a little bit harsh on freshmen, you know, kind of testing us, seeing if we were worthy to be there, verbally, so to speak.

Lee Roy, though—man, he was focused. Focused on what he was there for. He didn't treat the freshmen any differently. He wasn't so hard, in other words. He just went about business or football or school in a kind of quiet fashion. He did his talking out on the field, with action.

What made him such a good player? I think it was the way he was brought up. Everything starts at home, to me. We get influenced by our parents and our environment. When we're getting an education of life, we learn it all at home first, and Lee Roy, he had to come from a wonderful, hard-working family. He brought a good work ethic to school.

Coach Bryant recognized what kind of guy Lee Roy was and appreciated him for that. Sometimes I think Coach Bryant looked at Lee Roy as a younger version of himself. Their backgrounds were very similar.

I can't tell you how many times Coach Bryant singled out Lee Roy's style on the football field to talk about it. At football practice, I can remember Coach Bryant up in his tower saying, "Lee Roy! Go on in!" We'd all try to keep on practicing, but we couldn't help cutting a look over at Lee Roy.

To be excused from practice early, to be sent in off the practice field because you had done such a good job—I don't ever remember anyone being sent in from practice by Coach Bryant, other than Lee Roy Jordan, simply for doing a great job and giving such great effort on the practice field. That caught my eye and ear early on.

"Lee Roy! Go on in!" I never saw it happen to anybody else.

We have role models throughout our young lives at home, maybe at junior high school and high school. In college, though, the leadership you get at that level influences you the rest of your life. If you listen, if you pay attention, if you're fortunate enough to get good words of wisdom, it stays with you.

Lee Roy was a great leader on the football field and off the football field. My freshman year was when I really got to know him and appreciate him. He was respectful of everyone I ever saw him work with, and when it came to the younger players, he helped us out when he talked to us. He wanted us to go in the right direction, but you had to own up. If you wanted to emulate somebody in the way they carried themselves, Lee Roy would be the man.

We wound up in the NFL together, of course. I vaguely recall playing Dallas when Lee Roy was on the field, and I don't think we even looked each other in the eye. We might have once or twice, but it was all business.

As I said, he was highly focused. Or maybe I was too afraid to look at him.

I don't need to talk about Lee Roy's character off the field, because you already know that. I can't speak highly enough about the way Lee Roy conducts himself around people all the time. He is a class act in every way. He is a man, a gentleman, a man's man.

And, yes, he was tough on the football field. You know, I probably wouldn't be talking to you right now if I'd ever been hit by Lee Roy Jordan. I'm just glad I was his teammate, more importantly his friend!

Joe and I posed in front of a picture from the 1963 Orange Bowl. That is Joe throwing a pass while Cotton Clark (45) and I try to block an opponent.

INTRODUCTION

When I was growing up in the farming community of Excel, Alabama, in the 1940s and 1950s, I never dreamed that the game of football would pave the way for me to walk with some of the most famous people around, including governors, senators, writers, entertainers and even presidents of the United States.

When I was growing up, we got around riding wagons and on horses and mules until Dad bought an International truck in 1951, the year I turned 10. We didn't have electricity until I was 12, and that was when we finally got a radio. That's when I learned there was a world outside of Monroe County, Alabama.

That was also about the time that my brothers were playing high school football for the Excel Panthers. I was at practice one day watching, and the coach didn't have enough players to scrimmage, so he asked me to line up and play safety.

I didn't even have on a helmet but I made a tackle, which created a buzz.

I think the coaches just wanted me to be a "dummy" out there, not expecting me to participate in the scrimmage. The next day I was issued a helmet and football became a dominant part of my life.

Before I took my helmet off for the final time in 1976, I had been lucky enough to play for a couple of pretty famous football legends – Coach Paul Bryant and Coach Tom Landry – and on football fields with players who would help me be a national champion at Alabama and a Super Bowl winner for the Dallas Cowboys. I'd also be chosen as team captain by my teammates at both Alabama and Dallas, which was about as big an honor as a player could achieve.

There'd be some awfully famous games along the way from the warmth of the Orange Bowl in Miami to the Ice Bowl in Green Bay. There would be a lot of memorable victories and some awfully agonizing losses, too.

Football has played such a prominent role in my life, taking me to places that I never dreamed possible when I was a seventh-grader back in Excel. Yet, it has always been my family, faith and football that have defined my life. Without football, I'm not sure I would have lived as interesting a life. I know I would not trade it or the people I've met for anything else in the world.

My name is Lee Roy Jordan and this is my story.

One of my first football pictures as an Excel Panther.

CHAPTER 1
GROWING UP IN EXCEL, ALABAMA

My father, Walter Jordan, grew up in rural south Alabama, living like a lot of people back in the depths of the Depression days as a farmer.

My family were farmers who made a living off the land. We grew vegetables, cotton and peanuts. We also had cattle, hogs, chickens, horses, mules, you name it, we had it.

My mother was named Cleo and she was just as hard a worker as my father. I never knew anyone who got more done in a day's time that she did. She would cook three meals a day, and work on the farm just like the rest of us. At the end of the day, she would have picked more cotton than any of us.

To say I grew up in a big family would be an understatement.

I was one of seven children, and the fourth son. My oldest brother was Walter Junior and then came my sister Lottie, and brothers Carl and Benny Ray. I was born April 27, 1941 then came two younger sisters Agnes and Darlene.

That is me on the truck with my sister. My brothers Benny Ray and Carl.

One of the first tragedies in my life happened when Darlene was diagnosed with leukemia, and she would die tragically when she was only two.

My father and mother are the two people who instilled in me the importance of having honest character and a work ethic that would sustain me in my toughest times. When I got to Alabama in 1959 to play college football, Coach Bryant probably refined me but my parents are the ones who defined me.

My father had a strong Christian background and I'm proud to say that he was quick to tell me that he loved me and he would always hug me. When I would do something that he might not approve of, he would give me a "tune-up." I didn't get many of them, but when he gave me a "tune-up" I knew he wasn't too happy with me. My dad was a loving, caring man and he taught me to do the right things in life and how to treat people with proper respect and dignity.

Everybody who worked on our farm or any neighbor or cousins or anyone around was invited to a meal at my parents' table. My parents treated everyone with the same respect.

I started working when I was four years old and that was in 1945, the end of World War II. My first chores were to feed the chickens and pick peas, corn and cotton.

Tragedy would strike our family in 1948 when I was seven years old. The baby of our family, Darlene, became ill and the doctors really didn't know what was wrong with her. The news was grim when our family learned that she had leukemia.

It was heartbreaking for all of us. Since I was so young at the time, I probably didn't comprehend just how grave the situation had become, but I sensed the overwhelming grief that my parents were feeling.

In the 1940s, there wasn't any real cure for the disease, and she steadily got worse and worse. It was painful to watch her suffer and watch all my whole family suffer emotionally with her. There is really no better word to describe how we all felt other than devastated when she passed away. It scarred my folks for the rest of their lives.

I think our family's strong Christian faith and values sustained us during those dark days.

Church was a most important part of my upbringing. Our family belonged to the Assembly of God Church in Excel. We went to church every Sunday morning, Sunday night and Wednesday night. I was also a member of the boys' choir and enjoyed singing the traditional Christian hymns.

My parents were actively involved in the church, read the Bible to us, and always prayed their thanks for our blessings. There was never a meal when there wasn't a blessing of appreciation for all that we had.

When we lost Darlene, I can assure you the power of prayer helped my family endure the heartache we all felt. I do know we were all thankful for the time we had with her.

My father was a leader in our church, and it seemed that it didn't matter who the minister was, he would always lean on my dad and become friends with him.

One of our ministers and his wife became lifelong friends, not only of my parents but the entire Jordan family. His name is Carey Robertson, and I still talk to him and his wife Shirley regularly. They are still active in the ministry in south Mississippi, and they have traveled to 28 countries to deliver the message of Christianity.

While my family and church were the cornerstones of my life, so was education.

There was one school in Excel, first grade through the twelfth. It was a U-shaped building and I like to say I went in one end and came out the other. There were only 250 or so people who lived in Excel back then, so the classes were small. My class was actually one of the larger ones. There were 32 of us, which was a huge class by Excel standards.

I was a hard-working student, and one teacher who made sure that I understood the value of a good education was my English teacher. Mrs. Anna Laura Brown was the most impressive teacher I ever had. She made us understand she was pushing us, not for her benefit but for our own.

In a small school in a small town, your teachers stayed with you for years. Mrs. Brown taught me English from junior high until I graduated in 1959. Her impact on my life can't really be expressed in a few words, but I am forever grateful.

Monroe County is known as the "Literary Capital of Alabama," mainly because of two famous authors from Monroeville, Harper Lee and Truman Capote. I was a student at Alabama when *To Kill a Mockingbird* became a national best seller and won a Pulitzer Price for Harper Lee.

One of the thrills in my life was having the opportunity to meet and know her. She was a most gracious lady and it makes me feel proud that we came from the same county.

I know it's hard to comprehend now but we didn't have a motor vehicle until my dad bought an International pickup truck in the early 1950s. We got around on wagons pulled by mules and horses until then. I liked that truck and learned how to drive when I was 13. There were only dirt roads and I already knew how to drive a tractor, so driving the pickup was pretty easy for me.

We didn't have electricity until I was 12. I know it had to be a sight to see those old washtubs out in the yard and seeing my brothers and sisters pumping water in order to take a bath. We lived in a three-bedroom farmhouse until I was in high school, and it was a home where love and values were stressed.

My brothers, sisters, cousins and I worked hard but we had our diversions, too. There was a creek where we'd ride our horses to go fishing and swimming. We had some Tennessee walking horses, which are about the most graceful animal you'll ever see, and just fun to ride.

While they may have been easy to ride, that wasn't the case when we would have our own little rodeo. We'd get on steers and ride them, at least until they decided to throw us in the air.

I can remember Dad and a couple of his friends loading up and going to Houston, Texas, to look at cotton pickers. He bought the first ones ever used on a farm in south Alabama. That was a pretty futuristic purchase for the time and certainly made working the fields a lot easier. We had 480 acres, and most of those were devoted to cotton.

Obviously, we didn't have a television but when we got electricity, we bought a radio and that was an amazing piece of technology for us.

It helped us discover there was a world outside Excel, which is about seven miles from Monroeville. Excel was no bigger than a hiccup. We had only one four-way blinking light at the intersection going into town.

One year the town leaders decided it was time to go big-time and put up a full-fledged red, green and yellow light. It didn't stay up long because the Excel mayor figured out he didn't have enough money in the budget to pay for it. So, to us Monroeville was akin to going to the biggest city around.

They had a theater there, and it was quite a treat to go to watch movies. I liked the Western flicks, especially if John Wayne was starring in them. Never did I dream that I would not only meet him one day but I would become his friend as well.

I loved to listen to the radio and hear about things going on across the state of Alabama. Mobile was only 70 miles from Excel, but it seemed like a million to me. Even better was learning about things in faraway places like Georgia and Florida!

When I heard this young singer named Elvis, I had my first hero. I just loved listening to him, and still do. I'll be driving around today and turn the satellite radio to the Elvis channel and listen to him. There's no doubt the quality is certainly a lot better now than tuning to a station on an AM channel back in the 1950s!

Years later, probably in the late 1960s or early 1970s, my wife Biddie and I were in Las Vegas and we went to an Elvis Presley concert. He put on quite a show, a marathon really. He sang for three straight hours and I wanted to at least try to meet him and tell him that I was a fan.

So, I went to the dressing room area, and I told the security guard, "My name is Lee Roy Jordan and I play football for the Dallas Cowboys, and I'd really like Elvis to know how much I enjoyed his show."

The security man escorted me to meet him, and I'll never forget Elvis being there dressed in all white. He was sweating and had that towel wrapped around his neck. He couldn't have been more gracious but he was excited to meet me as well.

You know why? Because, he was a huge fan of Coach Bryant's and he wanted to know all about Coach Bryant! He was also a Dallas Cowboy fan and he had all kind of questions about our team.

I was in there for about 45 minutes and when I came out, Biddie and this other couple with us were not very happy I had told them to wait a few minutes and I'd get them in to meet him.

To this day Biddie has never forgiven me for not taking her in there to meet Elvis!

There's no doubt football is what paved my way not only to meet Elvis but a lot of other famous people.

My own football career began in the seventh grade when I was 12. My older brothers played, so I liked the game, even though my parents really weren't fans.

Anyway, I was watching practice one day, and there were only 21 players dressed out. The coach, Al Brandon, told me to stand out there where the safety was supposed to be, so he would have a complete defense.

I wasn't supposed to participate, other than occupy the space in the secondary, but when a running back broke through, I instinctively tackled him. It was the first one of my career, and I did it without a helmet.

The next day at practice, Coach Brandon issued me a helmet for the first time. I never dreamed football would become such a dominating part of my life for the next three decades.

When I was in high school, I played tailback, ran the ball, passed it, kicked and punted. On defense, I played linebacker. We only had two sports at Excel, football and basketball. I played forward on the basketball team, earning all-district honors. I was a pretty decent ball-handler and shooter but there was little doubt my real talent was on the football field.

I was lucky enough to have a high school coach, W.C. Majors, who would not only teach me how to play the game but more importantly would become a lifelong friend. He recognized that I had some talent and he pushed me every day to be a better player.

Coach Majors ran his drills like a boot camp. The practices were hard and intense, but they would serve me well, especially when I went off to college. His assistant coach was Joe Weaver and he would also become a lifelong mentor and friend.

Coach Weaver had a lot of confidence in me, and he helped me to understand the concept of teamwork and being a leader, not only on the field but off as well.

When I was in high school, there was a coaching change at Alabama, and it would ultimately change my life as well. Coach Majors would routinely travel to Tuscaloosa to attend clinics and learn more football from the new coach, Paul Bryant.

Before my junior year, I grew three inches and gained 30 pounds, and I added quite a bit of strength by lifting those hay bales on the farm. My whole world was getting ready to change, thanks to a coach named Jerry Claiborne coming to scout a player at W.S. Neal High School. I guess I was lucky that W.S. Neal just happened to be playing Excel, and I played well enough to get the attention of a young assistant at the University of Alabama.

I didn't think growing up in Excel was a very good thing when I was a child. Looking back on it, I was lucky to have had such a great family, including my brother Lee Roy. My parents were farmers and good Christian people. They taught all of us children the value of hard work, loyalty and nothing is given to you in life. You have to work for it.

Our main activity other than working on the farm was swimming at the creek and riding horses. We didn't have many toys, so we had a game called "Kick the Can." That's pretty corny now but we had fun doing it anyway.

I was lucky to have Lee Roy as a big brother. He and I were the babies and we just had a special bond. He was always protective of me, and looked after me when I was a child and still does. I think everyone learned early on that they better not mess with me or they had to go through Lee Roy.

Our parents really lived the Golden Rule and were leaders in the church. One minister, the Rev. Carey Robertson became part of our family and when our older brother was killed, he helped all of us make it through a most difficult time.

While family and church were important, so were athletics. I should have been a boy, because I loved sports and competing. Unfortunately, there were no girls sports back then, so I became a cheerleader and cheered Lee Roy's junior and senior year at Excel.

All of us had Coach Majors as a teacher but he was also the football coach, and we all loved him. He was great for Lee Roy, because he saw he had a special talent and knew he had a career in football.

My father didn't go to many games, because he was always worried Lee Roy would get hurt. I thought that was kind of ridiculous until my middle son played at Auburn, and I knew how my dad felt. My mother would go to the games to watch Lee Roy, but she really didn't understand much of anything about them.

We were at an Alabama game, and she started cheering for the team carrying the ball. I said, "Mom, Lee Roy is in the team in red that is trying to stop the team in white!"

While I would take my parents to some Cowboy games, the game I remember most was when he was at Alabama – his last game in the Orange Bowl against Oklahoma. It was pretty neat seeing your brother at the coin toss with President John Kennedy.

Think about it, how many people have that opportunity in life? It was exciting for me, so I can only imagine what Lee Roy thought.

What really was awesome was him making 31 tackles. He had made so many tackles at Excel and Alabama that it really didn't hit us until years later what he accomplished. When I sit back now and think about it, all I can do is say, "Wow, 31 tackles in one game. That's awesome."

I have to tell this one on Lee Roy as a kid. When we got a pickup truck, we would ride in the back, which is illegal now and probably was back then. My dad was driving toward our house, and Lee Roy was standing up in the back.

We had these mulberry trees along the road to the house, and this big limb hit him across the head and knocked him out of the truck.

He had to get stitched up and that was probably his hardest hit, including his days in football.

TIME OUT: JOE WEAVER

Joe Weaver served as a teacher, coach and bus driver at Excel High School from 1956-62. He and his wife Joyce became lifelong friends of Lee Roy Jordan. The Weavers are retired and live in Brewton, Alabama.

One of the greatest honors in my life was when Lee Roy Jordan told me that along with his father and Coach Bryant, I had been one of the people who had helped mold him into the man that he became. Being considered a second father to him is something that I truly cherish.

When my wife Joyce and I moved to Excel back in 1956, I helped Coach W.C. Majors with the football team. Coach Majors was a great head coach and I tried to help him build a winning program.

It wasn't easy because Excel was just a really small farming community, and we didn't have many players. The one young man who certainly stood out was Lee Roy Jordan. It was easy to see that he was good, but I don't think either Coach Majors or I dreamed that he would become one of the greatest players in the history of the state.

Lee Roy was an all-around football player, and we played him everywhere. He even played some quarterback at Excel, kicked, you name it, he did it. He was good enough that he started getting some attention from Auburn. Alabama became interested after the coaching change in Tuscaloosa and Coach Bryant took over.

Lee Roy's mother and father were farmers and had a big spread in Excel. They were getting older, and I think they envisioned Lee Roy taking over the farm and running it. So, naturally, Auburn appeared to be the school most likely to sign him.

And, I think Auburn was his favorite, but there were a couple of problems. Auburn had gotten placed on probation by the NCAA and one of the reasons was illegal inducements to married athletes.

Lee Roy was married for a short time while he was in high school, and I told Lee Roy that very well could be a problem if he went to Auburn. I know he had also become enamored with Coach Bryant and his vision for turning the Alabama program around.

You know we didn't make much money back in those days. I was making $2,300 a year, and I was asked if I would like to drive a bus and pick up a little more money. I asked how much and they said $65 a month, so I took the offer. One day when Lee Roy was a senior, the superintendent of the schools told me that I had to be in a faculty meeting on Friday and that I had to find a substitute bus driver. I recommended Lee Roy for that job.

Both the superintendent and principal thought it was a great idea. All the people in Excel loved Lee Roy, not because he was a star in athletics but because he was such a good person. He was always a yes sir and no sir man to grown-ups and the little kids loved him, because he always had time for them.

To this day, he still says yes sir and no sir to me and my wife. He was just brought up the right way in a fine Christian family.

In today's world, there's no way a student would drive a bus. Hey, none of them probably could, but Lee Roy had grown up driving farm equipment, so driving a school bus was easy for him. I never thought he'd have a problem and he didn't.

Anyway, I was waiting for him the day he arrived at the school in the bus, not because I was worried but because he was supposed to visit Auburn the next day.

I said, "Lee Roy, with the problems they've had with married students, I think you ought to think about Alabama."

I think he was worried that his parents would get upset because he felt they wanted him to go to Auburn and study agriculture. I told him that his parents only wanted what was best for him.

Obviously, he went on to become one of Alabama's and the Dallas Cowboys' all-time greats. I followed him through all those years he played with a great deal of pride and happiness that I had the opportunity to coach him. Any time you'd hear someone say they were from Excel, they would add, "That's the home of Lee Roy Jordan."

Back in those days when he was at Alabama, there weren't many games on TV and a lot of folks worked and didn't have the chance to listen. They'd come up to me and ask how Lee Roy was doing. I'd pretty much light up and say he's one of the best there is, and he was.

My wife pulled out the yearbook from Lee Roy's senior year in high school, the class of 1959. There is a picture in there of Coach Majors and me with Lee Roy. They dedicated the book to Coach Majors and me. That was flattering, but we both knew it was because of Lee Roy.

He'll always be the man who put Excel, Alabama on the football map.

Posed action shot of me at Alabama.

CHAPTER 2
EARNING A SCHOLARSHIP TO ALABAMA

Growing up in Excel had its advantages of being a close-knit community of around 250 people. It was and still is a blip on the map in Monroe County, and if you don't stray off the main back roads of Alabama, you aren't likely to find it.

One disadvantage was there weren't many youngsters from there that went off to college, and there had never been one to sign a football scholarship. It wasn't exactly a fertile recruiting territory for athletes. The thought of going to college or playing football on the next level never entered my mind until my junior year.

It was in the fall of 1957 that I found out for the first time that I might have an opportunity to do something no one in my family had ever done: go to college. My brothers had all joined either the Army or Navy after high school and my sister Lottie had moved to Mobile to be a secretary.

So, I thought I would follow in the footsteps of my older brothers, serve

My high school graduation picture in May, 1959.

my country and return to Excel to farm and ranch. That all changed when we played W.S. Neal in Brewton.

As I said earlier, Coach Jerry Claiborne was at the game to scout a player on the W.S. Neal team, and I guess I played well enough that he made a special trip to our locker room to tell my high school coaches that he would be back and that Alabama was going to recruit me.

We ran the single wing offense in high school, and I was the tailback. I remember running for a touchdown and throwing for one in the game; and I made a lot of tackles playing linebacker on defense and punted as well. There was a little blurb about me in the Brewton newspaper, and I guess that's the first time I had ever been recognized for playing well.

My senior football season was 1958 and there was an Alabama coach at every game, including Bobby Drake Keith and Gene Stallings. They were the main two who recruited me.

When I was growing up, obviously, there weren't many games on television and what I learned about college football came from the articles in the newspapers and reports on the radio. Mostly, though, our information came from our coaches.

I learned about Alabama and Auburn from them. Southern Miss showed interest in me as well. When I first started getting attention, Auburn was most interested and offered me a scholarship. Since my background was in agriculture, I really was interested in Auburn. They were also winning big at the time, and Alabama was in a down cycle.

I was a hard-working student who made good grades and I liked to learn about everything. One thing I learned was this new coach at Alabama was something special. Before he had come to Tuscaloosa, Auburn was dominating the state and the Tigers were coming off a national championship in 1957.

Auburn also went on probation and one of the reasons was they were providing extra benefits to players, especially to married players. When I was a senior, I had gotten married to my high school sweetheart, and I'm not sure if that affected Auburn's interest in me or not.

I don't know if that would have made any difference. I knew Coach Bryant had completely turned around the programs at Kentucky and Texas A&M, and I sensed he might not take long to do the same at Alabama.

In the fall of 1958, I was invited to attend a game in Tuscaloosa, and a friend of my family drove me there. Coach Bryant wanted to meet with him in his office early that morning, and I walked in there for the first time. There has been a lot written about his presence, including that famous quote from his quarterback at Kentucky and all-time NFL great George Blanda who said, "When I first saw him, I thought that must be what God looks like."

I know one thing; Coach Bryant made quite an impression. He had an air of confidence about him that few people have. I'd never been around a person before or since that that had just an overwhelming presence like Coach Bryant. Anyone who was ever lucky enough to be in his office can appreciate this. He was a big, powerful man and he became even more intimidating because the couch in his office was lower than his desk, and you just sank about four inches when you sat down!

He started telling me about the university and getting an education, and

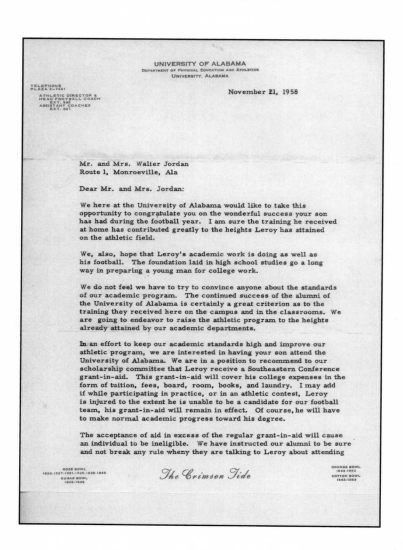

University of Alabama letter, November 21, 1958:

UNIVERSITY OF ALABAMA
Department of Physical Education and Athletics
University, Alabama

TELEPHONE
PLAZA 2-7441

ATHLETIC DIRECTOR &
HEAD FOOTBALL COACH
EXT. 642
ASSISTANT COACHES
EXT. 641

November 21, 1958

Mr. and Mrs. Walter Jordan
Route 1, Monroeville, Ala

Dear Mr. and Mrs. Jordan:

We here at the University of Alabama would like to take this opportunity to congratulate you on the wonderful success your son has had during the football year. I am sure the training he received at home has contributed greatly to the heights Leroy has attained on the athletic field.

We, also, hope that Leroy's academic work is doing as well as his football. The foundation laid in high school studies go a long way in preparing a young man for college work.

We do not feel we have to try to convince anyone about the standards of our academic program. The continued success of the alumni of the University of Alabama is certainly a great criterion as to the training they received here on the campus and in the classrooms. We are going to endeavor to raise the athletic program to the heights already attained by our academic departments.

In an effort to keep our academic standards high and improve our athletic program, we are interested in having your son attend the University of Alabama. We are in a position to recommend to our scholarship committee that Leroy receive a Southeastern Conference grant-in-aid. This grant-in-aid will cover his college expenses in the form of tuition, fees, board, room, books, and laundry. I may add if while participating in practice, or in an athletic contest, Leroy is injured to the extent he is unable to be a candidate for our football team, his grant-in-aid will remain in effect. Of course, he will have to make normal academic progress toward his degree.

The acceptance of aid in excess of the regular grant-in-aid will cause an individual to be ineligible. We have instructed our alumni to be sure and not break any rule wheny they are talking to Leroy about attending

ROSE BOWL
1926-1927-1931-1935-1938-1946
SUGAR BOWL
1945-1948

The Crimson Tide

ORANGE BOWL
1943-1953
COTTON BOWL
1942-1954

Mr. and Mrs. Walter Jordan   Page 2

the University. If you hear of any one of our alumni doing anything
illegal when they are talking to your son, I wish you would bring it to
the attention of one of my coaches or myself.

Needless to say, we hope Leroy decides to attend the University of
Alabama. We know he will help us to have a better University and,
also, know the University will prepare him to face life upon graduation.

Looking forward to meeting you personally, I am

Sincerely yours,

Paul Bryant

Paul W. Bryant
Director of Athletics

PWB:mp

how I was the type of player who would fit into his plan. His plan was pretty
simple: he was going to restore Alabama to a championship level again. Then he
wanted to know if he offered me a scholarship would I accept it. Even if I had
wanted to tell him I was not coming, there was no way I could turn him down,
and I probably just mumbled, "Yes sir, I'd be here."

I don't remember much about the game but I was pretty happy to have become one of the first persons ever from Excel, Alabama, to earn a football scholarship.

A few weeks later, my parents received an official letter from Coach Bryant offering me a scholarship. I have kept that letter ever since. I still have to laugh a little bit because Coach spelled my name Leroy. It really didn't make much difference to me how he spelled it or what he called me!

My parents were thrilled, not because they cared much for football, but because I was the first person from our family to be able to go college. Here's the letter that they received from Coach Bryant.

Recruiting is so different now than it was back then. There wasn't much hoopla around it. Coach Keith drove up to my house and we signed the papers to go to the university.

There was quite a celebration in our household though, and like I said my folks really weren't football fans.

They were deeply religious and I don't know if they cared much for the sport. When my brothers and I played for the Excel Panthers, they would come to some games but not all of them. Years later when I was with the Cowboys, they'd come to Dallas to see me play. That was a milestone moment for them to travel that far to see a game.

MOVING TO TUSCALOOSA

My freshman class was truly blessed with not only some good football players but even better people and unbelievable leaders, men like Bill Battle, Richard Williamson, Butch Wilson and Mike Fracchia.

Coach Bryant assigned me to live with Richard, probably because he was from Fort Deposit, which is close to Excel. I think Coach knew that it was the first time for most of us to be away from our families, and he thought we'd be better served rooming with players from our same region.

I wasn't sure what position I would play but it didn't take Coach Bryant long to tell me that I was going to be a center-linebacker. I'd never played center in my life, but one thing I had done throughout high school was to play every snap, including the kicking games. Back in those days, because of the limited substitution rules, you hardly left the field.

And, for that reason, you had to be in unbelievable physical shape to run for 60 minutes. I learned playing for Coach Bryant, there was no lollygagging around. You played and ran hard every play in every practice and every game, or you weren't going to be around very long.

People like to say football back then was survival of the fittest, and I think that was definitely true at Alabama. We were Coach Bryant's second class, and we might not have had it as tough as the first group of freshmen, but I can't imagine it being any worse.

Sometimes we would practice for three-and-a-half hours without a water break. No one knew anything about dehydration in the 1950s, and I can remember players just dragging themselves back to the locker room.

I think we all thought about quitting at one time or another, but my parents didn't teach me to quit, so whenever those thoughts would enter my mind, they didn't last too long. I could hear my father's and mother's voices telling me, "Don't quit."

Every day I adapted and bought into Coach Bryant's philosophy of "being the best you can be." He had an amazing capacity to know how far to push you, convincing you to reach your potential, even to a level you could never imagine reaching.

He did it to the team, declaring in the meetings, "If you work hard, we will have a championship team and we'll have it soon."

And we believed him.

The core of players who stayed got closer and closer each day. We built stamina and toughness, and I think a desire to never let Coach Bryant down. I think that was an unwritten rule that all his players and coaches shared. You just didn't want to let this man down.

We lived in Friedman Hall and I think the players living together helped build a bond that lasted a lifetime. Not many of us had very much as far as material things went, but we had a desire to get an education and win a championship.

When I got to Tuscaloosa from Excel, I had a little hand-me-down bag with my all my clothes, three shirts and three pairs of blue jeans. And I thought I was the luckiest kid around, just being able to be at the university and play football for Coach Bryant.

I don't know if anyone has the real ability to describe Coach Bryant. He made the players believe. Believe in him, believe in themselves, believe in their teammates. He made us believe we could win.

He talked about the importance of character and work ethic, and he pushed us to a level I don't think anyone of us knew existed. He had the unique knack of making you want to improve in all aspects of your life, not just in football. He made us write home to our parents, thanking them for what they'd done for us.

I can assure you when he came around and asked us if we had written home, you better believe I had.

He made us appreciate our teachers in the classroom for providing us with an opportunity to earn a first-class education. He made us appreciate a teammate who might not be as gifted but who gave every ounce of effort to make the team better. It was always about the team to him.

A great team has one heartbeat, he'd say, and we knew what he meant. We all shared it.

There were so many things I admired about Coach Bryant but none more than how he took up for his players and coaches. When we lost, he accepted all the blame, saying it was his fault. When we won, it was the team that did it.

I think I learned more about leadership from Coach Bryant than anyone else. He knew there were players who responded well to a pat on the back and others who needed to get pushed in a different manner. I hope I developed some of that when I was a player and later when I had my business.

During my rookie year with Dallas there were some players who I didn't think were giving it their all at practice, and I got on them. Some of the veterans weren't too happy with me, because rookies weren't supposed to be vocal. I had learned to lead by example but I had also learned not to hesitate to be speak up when players weren't doing what was best for the team.

At Alabama, freshmen weren't eligible to play for the varsity in 1959. That didn't mean we weren't learning what it meant to win and how to be leaders. I know Coach Bryant helped me to become a leader and to try to be one on and off the field.

TIME OUT: BOBBY DRAKE KEITH

Bobby Drake earned two degrees from Texas A&M. After being one of Paul Bryant's legendary "Junction Boys," he would serve as an assistant coach at Alabama, Texas A&M and Oklahoma. He is one of the few coaches to have worked for both Coach Bryant and Oklahoma legend Bud Wilkinson. Although he went into the business world in 1965, he still follows football and remembers the day he signed a recruit from Excel, Alabama.

After I played at Texas A&M, I joined Coach Bryant on his original staff at Alabama. Jerry Claiborne, who had played for Coach Bryant at Kentucky and then was an assistant at A&M when I was playing, had watched a young player named Lee Roy Jordan and thought he might be a prospect.

Coach Bryant sent me to watch Lee Roy play to get a second opinion. Frankly I thought he was what they call today "a tweener." We had a color code system for recruits back then. A blue player was the best, meaning we thought he would be good enough to start by his sophomore year. Freshmen weren't eligible back then and if you thought a player could start by his sophomore year that meant he was pretty good in our eyes.

A red player was somebody we thought might start at some time and a white was a player that we thought may or may not play, but we'd take a chance on him. I thought Lee Roy was probably in that red or white category. We certainly didn't think he was a blue.

We decided to make an offer to Lee Roy and I drove to Excel to let him know we wanted him at Alabama. I was actually on my way to Mobile where there was a player we wanted more than him. Well, I got to the high school and went to the principal's office to find Lee Roy. I had never met him in person.

I'll never forget those oily floors at the school and in the principal's office. They were covered with sawdust, which was pretty common back in the 1950s. When I told the principal I wanted to see Lee Roy, he told me that he wasn't in school that day, that he was home working. It was also not unsual in the farming communities for the boys to stay home and work.

The principal told me how to get out to Lee Roy's house, and I drove out there and saw a young man on a tractor. I figured that had to be Lee Roy, so I pulled up to the fence and got out of the car. Lee Roy drove up on the tractor, got off and we introduced ourselves. I told him we wanted him at Alabama.

It was the only time I ever recruited a player driving a tractor and offered him a scholarship while standing on the other side of a fence!

Back in those days, Coach Bryant wanted to sign the players at 12:01 a.m., the earliest they could sign. The coaches usually were there to sign the top prospects and I was in Mobile, signing a player whom we rated higher than Lee Roy.

It wasn't against the rules then to have a supporter help in recruiting and there was an Alabama fan in Monroeville, Bud Lathram, who went to make sure Lee Roy signed. I wasn't there to sign the best player I'd ever recruit and one of the greatest football players ever.

I went back to Texas A&M after the 1959 season to finish my degrees in geology and petroleum engineering, so I didn't know how well Lee Roy was doing. Games weren't on television very much. But by 1961, everyone in college football knew his name.

I came back to Alabama as an assistant in 1962, Lee Roy's senior year. We had a great team, finishing 10-1 and beating Oklahoma 17-0 in the Orange Bowl. We also shut out Auburn for the fourth straight year.

I'll never forget the PA announcer at Legion Field during the Auburn game. College football had some crazy substitution rules back then, and you could only sub a handful of players. Auburn had the ball near our goal line late in the game and the announcer said, "And going in for Alabama is Lee Roy Jordan."

Auburn didn't score with Lee Roy in there.

My last game at Alabama was the Orange Bowl against Oklahoma. Ironically, I joined Bud Wilkinson's staff for the 1963 season soon after the game. Of course, the buzz around Miami on New Year's Day was about President John Kennedy being in attendance and Joe Namath becoming known across the country.

But it was a day that belonged to Lee Roy Jordan. He put on one of the greatest defensive performances ever, making 31 tackles and completely shutting down the OU offense. When I joined the Oklahoma staff, their coaches didn't want to talk about the president or Joe Namath. All they wanted to talk about was Lee Roy Jordan.

My best friend in high school was a great football player named Jerry Tubbs. He went on to star for Oklahoma and the Dallas Cowboys as a middle linebacker. When Dallas drafted Lee Roy in the first round in 1963, Jerry took him under his wing and let everyone know that this young guy was brought into be his replacement, and he would be for the next 14 years

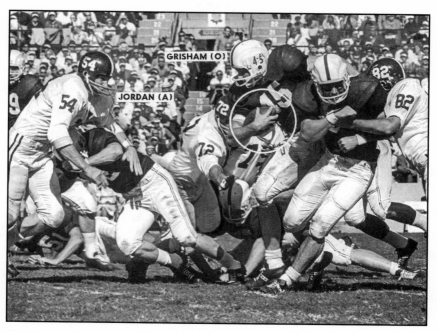

This is one of my 31 tackles in the Orange Bowl.

Coach Bryant and I pose before the 1961 championship season.

CHAPTER 3
LEARNING THE COACH BRYANT WAY

When I got to Alabama in the fall of 1959, I heard all the horror stories from upperclassmen about how hard it was going to be, and they were right. There really was no way to describe how intense those August practices were, and like it's been told again and again, there were players always leaving.

I'd be lying to say the thought didn't cross my mind a time or two, but I was determined to make it, and I really think one of the reasons was the bond that developed with my fellow freshmen of that year.

We'd go back to the dormitory and uplift each other, and I believed in the coaching staff, particularly Coach Bryant. He told us we were going to be champions, and he wasn't just talking about winning the Southeastern Conference either.

They had already endured a year of the sacrifices that Coach Bryant expected from players to develop into a championship team.

While being subjected to a new level of just gut-wrenching, hard-nosed practices, it didn't take long for me to see that those guys who had made it through the 1958 season were a tough bunch of men.

I think about Jim Blevins. He'd been in the military, and I think you could ask every player who was the toughest guy on the team, and they'd tell you Jim Blevins. He'd hit you like a hammer, and I felt if I could survive going against him, then I could play against anybody.

Since we weren't eligible to participate in varsity games, playing the freshmen games was fun, and I'd adapted to being a center for the first time. Back when everyone played two ways, centers were linebackers on defense. The same for fullbacks. From day one, the coaches wanted to make me a center, and they assigned me the number 54.

Never in my life would I think that number would forever become such a part of Alabama folklore, but even today, it's humbling when fans remember that was my college number.

By the time we opened the 1960 season against Georgia and their stellar quarterback Fran Tarkenton, I was listed as the starter at center and linebacker. Charley Pell was the only other Bama sophomore in the starting lineup that day at Legion Field in Birmingham. I don't know if it registered with either one of us, but it wasn't commonplace for a sophomore to start at an SEC school in 1960.

When I was playing at Excel, they'd have a few hundred fans in the stadium, so walking into the stadium that day with a crowd of more than 60,000 and with the game being nationally televised, well that was something really special.

We had two really good quarterbacks in 1960, senior Bobby Skelton and junior Pat Trammell. Bobby was just a really good athlete who would go on to a long and prestigious career as an NFL official. I'll talk more about Pat later, but he was one of the toughest, most hard-nosed players you can ever imagine.

While those two really were an effective tandem that year, Georgia had one of the greatest quarterbacks of all time in Tarkenton. For fans too young to remember him, Fran was Johnny Manziel before Johnny Manziel.

He was like chasing lightning in a bottle, and he could throw the heck out of the football as well. The year before he had led the Bulldogs to a 17-3 victory over Alabama in Athens, and Georgia was favored to win this game as well. They also had a senior guard named Pat Dye who went on to become a successful assistant coach at Alabama and head coach at Auburn.

For Coach Bryant, there were no excuses for not being prepared. There was no substitute for preparation, and we were ready. In *The Birmingham News* the morning of the game, Coach Bryant was quoted as saying, "We might not win, but we are not going to beat ourselves."

I've never seen a coach who had that knack of getting the best effort out of his players and having them completely ready to compete, and we were that day. After a scoreless first quarter, we scored three touchdowns in the second quarter. Skelton engineered all the drives, scoring twice on short runs and handing off to Leon Fuller for the third. We were up 21-0 at the half.

You never knew what to expect from Coach Bryant at halftime, and he told us he wasn't too happy. We are thinking, "If he's not happy with that half, I'd hate to see him if we were behind." We were up on Georgia 21-0 and we hadn't played well? I know now he was just making sure we didn't let down in the second half, and we really didn't.

We didn't score again but we completely shut down Fran and the Georgia offense. They ran a punt back down near our goal line and scored a touchdown in the final seconds on a Tarkenton pass. The final score was 21-6, and I think we showed everyone that Alabama was going to be a factor, not only in 1960 but for years to come.

There would be some forgettable days in 1960 as well, including a 6-6 tie against a Tulane team that would finish the season 3-6-1. They were far from being a bad team, and they lost a lot of close games that year, and should have lost a close one to us.

That was my first trip to New Orleans, and it was like all of our road trips, a business trip. Tulane Stadium was where the Sugar Bowl had always been played, and it was the biggest stadium I'd ever seen.

We fell behind 6-0 and it stayed that way until the final minutes when Pat Trammell scored a touchdown to tie it up, but we had a bad snap on the extra point, and I don't think Tommy Brooker even got the kick off.

Let me tell you, Coach Bryant was none too happy with the way we had played, and he called one of his infamous Sunday practices. We scrimmaged just like it was a game, until he felt like we had learned our lesson about taking another team lightly.

We sure didn't take Tennessee lightly that Third Saturday in October in Knoxville, but we certainly played one of our worst games of my three years. In the first quarter, we fumbled on the first play of the game, and they recovered near our goal line and scored a couple of plays later.

Then we fumbled again, and they ran it in for another score, and then there was another turnover, and we were down 20-0. Leon Fuller scored for us to make it 20-7, but we lost some more turnovers and never could get back in the game.

Defensively, we had one of our best games of the year, holding the Volunteers to five first downs and a total of 108 yards. It's hard to believe you can lose when you do that, but it just illustrates the importance of ball security.

I don't even think Tennessee made a first down in the second half. It had to be one of the most frustrating days of Coach Bryant's coaching career. I know as a player it was a game that we knew we had the better team, but we just flat gave it away.

Later in the season, we had our annual grudge game against Georgia Tech, and it would be a game that really proved to us that we were developing the mentality of being champions.

It was a game that Coach Bryant really enjoyed, because the Yellow Jackets were well coached by Bobby Dodd.

Coach Bryant would use that speech of his, saying their talent level was 85 out of 100, and ours was 75 out of 100, but if they play at 85 and we play at 100, then we will win the game.

We were playing hard in the first half, but it wasn't doing us much good as we fell behind 15-0. I figured Coach Bryant was really going to jump on us pretty hard at halftime, but he didn't. He told us we had them right where we wanted them and that we would go out there and shut them out in the second half and score enough points to win it.

I believed in Coach Bryant, but I don't know how many of us thought it was possible. None of us ever wanted to let him down, though, so we went out there and played every play 100 percent, just like we had been taught.

Late in the third quarter, Pat Trammell drove us down the field for a score, but our attempt for two failed, so going into the fourth quarter, we were down 15-6. And Pat had gotten hurt, so it was up to Bobby Skelton to try to lead us to an improbable victory, and it looked pretty bleak when we were backed up on our 13 and not much time left.

Coach Bryant had told us we were going to win the game in the fourth quarter, and I think that's the day the tradition of the Crimson Tide players raising their four fingers to signify the fourth quarter is ours began.

We believed the fourth quarter was ours, that we were mentally and physically tougher than our opponents, and we were that day in Atlanta. Three different times we converted on fourth down, and Bobby completed a three-yard TD pass to Norbie Ronsonet. After the extra point, we were down 15-13.

Our defense held Tech and forced a punt, which backed us up to our 20, with only a minute or so to play. With time running out, Bobby completed a long pass to Butch Wilson to the Tech six-yard line, and we rushed our field goal team on the field to try to win it.

Our regular kicker Tommy Brooker had gotten hurt, so Digger O'Dell ran onto the field for the only field goal attempt of his career. When the football sailed through the uprights, it set off a wild celebration on our sideline, and I think we all knew then the magic of Coach Paul Bryant was indeed real.

A few weeks later, I played in my first Iron Bowl, and talk about being special. Legion Field was known as The Football Capital of the South, and seeing the crowd of 68,000 split right down the middle, half wearing crimson and white and the other half orange and blue, added to the entire carnival-like atmosphere in Birmingham.

Auburn was ranked No. 6 in the country coming into the game, and we knew it would be a knock-down, drag-out fight. In the second quarter, Brooker kicked a field goal to give us a 3-0 lead. Tommy was still injured and didn't have on shoulder pads when he trotted out to kick what would be the game's only points.

We totally dominated their offense in the second half, holding them to one first down and intercepting their quarterback Bobby Hunt three times. I was fortunate enough to pick off one of the passes. Leon Fuller and Bobby Skelton got the other two.

Our reward for an 8-1-1 season was an invitation to play Texas in the first-ever Bluebonnet Bowl in Houston. That was another defensive struggle that ended in a 3-3 tie, and I was voted the defensive player of the game, earning me a trophy of some sort. I'm pretty sure it was the first time I was ever formally recognized by the press for my play.

That was a disappointing tie because we felt we had scored a touchdown in the first quarter when Bobby Skelton was called down, literally on the inch line. Bobby always said he scored. That was a third-down play. On fourth down, we went for it and Billy Richardson was ruled down at the same spot. Bobby was even more adamant that Billy had crossed the goal line.

Regardless, the score remained 3-3, and we went back to Tuscaloosa with one thing on our minds, getting ready for the 1961 season.

It would certainly be one of my favorite seasons, as our team returned the Crimson Tide to the pinnacle of the college football world.

CHAPTER 4
THE SPECIAL BOND OF THE 1961 TEAM

A lot is made about the unlimited signing of players across the country back in the 1950s and early 1960s, but little is said about how few survived the rigors of making it and playing college football. In the spring of 1961, we had a total of 69 players on the entire roster, with 14 of them being seniors. Only eight were players from Coach Bryant's first class and the other six had either transferred in or had been on campus when Coach arrived. We had survived to be part of what turned out to be one of the most important years in my life.

I think collectively we felt like we were on the verge of being a special football team. I know it was a special time in my life, not only for being part of a championship environment but I had met my future wife, Biddie Banks, in a biology class at Alabama.

Biddie's mother and grandmother were both named Mary, and her given name is Mary Haymond Banks, but everyone called her Little Biddie Mary and the name stuck. Biddie grew up in the small town of Eutaw, which is southwest of Tuscaloosa in Greene County. Her family was in the hardware, furniture and lumber business.

There were a few football players in the biology class with her, and I like to kid her that she was flirting with one of my teammates when I stepped in. I kind of knew that we were going to be married.

Life off the football field was pretty simple back then. We went to a little restaurant in east Tuscaloosa called the Jungle Club on our first date, and she ordered a beer and I ordered a coke. The waiter put the beer in front of me, and I told him he had it wrong. I had never been exposed to much drinking.

We were married in 1964 and she has been the love of my life for more than 52 years, the mother of our three sons and the grandmother of our eight grandchildren.

She was a great influence on me immediately, and if I needed any more inspiration to perform well in all phases of my life, she provided it.

On the football field, Coach Bryant challenged us to be champions. I can still hear him telling us, "There is little difference in being average and being a champion. A champion has a winning attitude on and off the field. Take pride in everything you do."

Before I talk about the 1961 season, here are some facts about that staff and team. I really don't know if there has ever been a better coaching staff where two of the assistants, Howard Schnellenberger and Gene Stallings, would go on to win national championships as head coaches.

Then there was Pat James, who had a legendary career as an assistant at Alabama, LSU and Oklahoma. He might have been as good an assistant as anyone, and I know he was one of the toughest men I have ever known.

Years later, I heard him tell the story about talking to Coach Bryant before the season. Coach asked Pat if he thought we had a chance to be any good that fall. Coach James was in awe of Coach Bryant like the rest of us. He had played for him at Kentucky and started his coaching career at Texas A&M.

Pat said, " I looked at Coach Bryant and told him as long as Lee Roy is in the game, we are going to be hard to beat."

There's no doubt that still makes me proud, but I can assure you he didn't tell me that during my playing days for him.

The 1961 team had the best group of leaders I've ever seen collected at one time on a football field. I don't think there is any question during those days when you played both ways that Coach Bryant relied on the quarterbacks to lead the offense and the middle linebacker to lead the defense.

Pat Trammell, was one of the best leaders I've ever been around. Coach Bryant loved Pat Trammell. He would do anything in his physical power to win. He was one of those players who refused to lose. He was the perfect match for Coach Bryant.

I tried my best to lead by being totally prepared for every play, not only in the games but in practice. I was lucky to be blessed with some talent and instincts, but I believed in what Coach Bryant constantly preached, and that was playing hard all the time and being totally prepared.

The 1961 team was loaded with leaders and great people. Of those 69 there in the spring, we knew with the substitution rules that only 30 or so would play in a game during the 1961 season. Of the players who played the most in 1961, two would become doctors, one a dentist and two athletic directors.

Five of them became college head coaches and 16 became presidents of companies. We even had an entertainer, lawyers and stock brokers as well. The football team had the highest scholastic grade point average of any organization on campus. It was a special group.

The success we had on the football field would sustain us throughout our lives. All the elements were in place for us. We were the best-conditioned team I think there has ever been. We didn't lift weights back then, but we ran and ran and ran. We did quickness drills and worked endlessly on fundamentals. We were not going to beat ourselves.

Coach Bryant made us confident, pushed us to the limit of our physical and mental abilities, and built the great oneness of a team with the one heartbeat. I know I wanted nothing more than to please Coach Bryant, and I think that's how all of us felt who made it.

He had a magical touch, and he made us believe. He preached to us that every game came down to six or seven plays, and you don't know when they are coming, but do your job on every play to make sure the play goes our way.

Coach Bryant demanded that you be better than you thought you were. He had the ability to push you to the brink where you didn't think you could go on. Then, he'd put his arm around you and say, "I'm just trying to make you a better player and person." And you were ready to do whatever he commanded.

One of my old coaches, Dude Hennessey summed it up best when asked about Coach Bryant: "The one word for him is father. He was the second father to the players and his coaches."

We players developed a brotherhood on and off the field that would last a lifetime. Years after the 1961 season, Coach Schnellenberger, who coached the 1983 championship team at Miami and was on the staff of the 1972 Miami Dolphins' unbeaten team, said, "Coach Bryant made it like a marine boot camp. The ones that remained developed a pride in themselves and their teammates.

"It wasn't a really talented team. The 1961 team was a collection of ordinary players but what they went through together built that brotherhood among them that lasted well after their playing days. Coach Bryant molded this team into being like him. They played harder than they ever thought they could and harder than any team I've ever seen.

"They were an elite group of young men who developed that esprit de corps that made them unbeatable."

Our bond was just as strong off the field as it was when we were playing. We had our lighter moments. One of those came when my mother baked me a pecan pie and I took it back to Tuscaloosa. As I said earlier, I still think my mother is the best cook that ever lived, and my favorite of all her dishes was her pecan pie.

I still love eating a good piece of pecan pie, but to this day, I've never come close to having any like my mother's.

Anyway, I brought the pie back to the dorm where I was rooming with Richard Williamson. When I come back to the room, the pie is gone! Richard swore to me that he didn't eat the pie, and I believed him. I knew that there was another culprit on the team.

Years later, my good friend Mal Moore confessed that he was the one who ate the pie. He just smiled that impish grin of his and we had a good laugh over it. I asked him why it took so long for him to confess, and he said he didn't want me to take it out on him on the practice field.

At least, I finally knew what happened to my pie!

On the field, life couldn't have been much better. As Coach Bryant told his staff, "I think we are aimed and coiled to do something special." And, I think that's how we really felt when we came back in August and started getting ready for our opener against Georgia in Athens.

TIME OUT: BROTHER OLIVER

Brother Oliver was a teammate of Lee Roy Jordan on the 1961 national championship team and has remained a lifelong friend. A member of the State of Alabama Sports Hall of Fame, Oliver went on a distinguished career as a defensive coordinator.

Having been a member of Coach Bryant's first signing class, I think we could all see a distinct improvement in talent when he had a full year to recruit his 1959 class. There were some really good players in that group, players like Butch Wilson and Mike Fracchia, but the one who stood out to all of us was Lee Roy Jordan.

One day I was feeling pretty good because Coach Bryant had bragged about me having a good practice. I had recovered from a torn cartilage injury to my rib cage and was feeling pretty good about myself.

The next day we were scrimmaging when Lee Roy laid it on me. I had never fumbled in a game or in practice, until that day. We were down on the goal line and ran a play called "Over 45." As soon as I got the ball, I got hit by Lee Roy. He hit me so hard, the ball went one way and my helmet the other.

I was laid out, lost my breath. Coach Bryant stood over me and said, "I thought you were a player." All I could think was there was no player who wanted to be tackled by Lee Roy Jordan, friend or foe!

Let me tell you something about Lee Roy: He was one smart player. He called all of our defenses for three years at Alabama and he did the same for the Dallas Cowboys. Put that in perspective. It's a like a quarterback calling his own plays for 17 straight seasons.

He was really a genius at calling defensive signals, getting players in the right position. The other thing that made him so great was he was the most instinctive player I've ever seen. He just knew where the ball was going. He didn't have great size but he had quickness and a God-given knack of knowing where the football was going.

Coach Bryant was so far ahead of any other coach it's hard to describe, and Lee Roy was the perfect player for him. We were doing things defensively in the 1960s that a lot of schools didn't get around to doing until years later. And, I know Lee Roy spent a lot of those early years working with Coach Jerry Claiborne to learn every nuance of our defensive system.

Lee Roy is a leader, and a man's man on and off the field. His parents instilled a work ethic in him that made him prepare harder than any other player. If you listen to him speak, he talks about things he learned growing up in Excel. Lee Roy has always stood for the right things. He's just a high-principled man.

On the playing field, he'd grab players by the bootstraps and say, "Let's go." And, they'd go. People knew he walked the walk, gave everything he had on every play of every practice and every game, so it was easy to follow his lead.

When Coach Bryant said, "If he stays inbounds, Lee Roy will get him," he meant it because it was true. I don't know how many tackles he made in his career, but I doubt many players in the history of the game have made any more than him.

After I completed my football eligibility at Alabama in 1961, I went out and played for the baseball team and was around to watch Lee Roy in his senior year and in the all-star games that followed.

A group of his old teammates gathered around the TV in the summer of 1963 to watch the College All-Star Game matching the best players from college against the NFL champion Green Bay Packers.

On a critical third-and-short play, Lee Roy broke through the Packer offensive line and hit Green Bay fullback Jimmy Taylor in the backfield, dropping him for a loss. The announcers went wild because no one tackled Taylor for a loss, but all of us had seen him do the same thing at Alabama so many times that nothing he did surprised us. Lee Roy made that play. Heck, he always made the play. He was the ultimate playmaker.

Few people know that we almost went to the Rose Bowl. This is me with our trainer Jim Goostree getting a taste of sugar.

CHAPTER 5
FULFILLING THE DREAM OF BEING NO. 1

We'd finished 8-1-2 in 1960, and we felt like we should have won every game, so I think there was a feeling among the entire team that we were going to win the championship in 1961. It was what Coach Bryant promised and preached to us: "Do the little things and we will win the national championship."

Actually, we were a junior-dominated team but we had great senior leadership, particularly in the two captains, Pat Trammell and Billy Neighbors. Billy was one of the best blockers I ever saw, period. He had tremendous leverage on every play, was strong and had unbelievable blocking technique. He played every play of the game, and he would always be the highest-graded player of the week by the coaches.

He was also a great defensive player. The defensive linemen were taught to take on the blockers and keep them from getting to the linebackers, and that certainly helped Darwin Holt and me make a lot of tackles in that championship year.

If there was ever a player born to play for Coach Bryant and represent him on the field it was Pat Trammell. He was a born leader, a fierce competitor, tough as hell, and wouldn't back down from anybody, including Coach Bryant.

I think that's why Coach Bryant trusted him and loved him so much. He had the iron resolve to win, just like Coach Bryant, and left everything he had on the football field. He would almost will the team to do well at practice and in the games, and with him in the lineup, you knew you always had a chance to win.

And we won them all in 1961. After that year, Pat graduated and entered the university's medical school where he excelled, just like everyone expected. I'll never forget after my senior year, I was invited to play in the Senior Bowl in Mobile, and on one play, I got slammed pretty hard in the mouth, bad enough for me to lose four front teeth.

When I got back to Tuscaloosa, I went by to see Coach Bryant, and he got on the telephone and called the dental school in Birmingham and told them he was sending me up there to get my teeth fixed. Well, I am sitting in the dentist's chair not feeling too good when Pat comes into the room.

He's got three of his fellow medical students with him, and they wanted to meet me. It was quite a sight, because Pat was making fun of the way I looked, and I can understand why. Over the next few years when I'd come back from Dallas, I'd see Pat on occasion. He was finishing up his medical degree and preparing for his career as a doctor.

When Pat was diagnosed with cancer, we were all shocked but I think all his old teammates believed that he would get well, mainly because he was Pat Trammell and if anybody could beat the cancer, it would be Pat.

Pat died the week after the Auburn game in 1968. He was able to attend the Iron Bowl, and the team gave him the game ball after Alabama won 24-16. I know his death was a devastating blow to Coach Bryant, and really to all of us who knew him. I think all of his teammates just think of what he could have accomplished in his life if he had not died at the age of 28.

Before I talk about the 1961 season, I want to talk about a reunion with Coach Bryant in the 1970s. We were sitting around and Coach Bryant said he was going to start a scholarship to help take care of his former players' children and Pat's children would get their education from the University through this Bryant Scholarship. He said it would be a small way to repay his players for what they did for him.

Through the ensuing years thousands of young men and women, the children of Coach Bryant's former players, have attended the University of Alabama on this scholarship. Paul Bryant Junior still manages the funds for his father. I think it is a lasting tribute to the greatness of Coach Bryant and his concern for his former players and their children.

The 1961 team re-established Alabama as a dominating power in college football, a position it had first held back during those Rose Bowl years with Coach Wallace Wade and then with Coach Frank Thomas, the man most responsible for the football career of Coach Bryant.

We opened the year at Georgia and won easily 32-6 with Mike Fracchia displaying his enormous skills at running back. John Forney, the fabled "Voice of the Crimson Tide," liked to tell the story about us getting off the bus and walking through a maze of Georgia fans who were trying to harass us.

John recalled it like this: "If they thought they could intimidate guys like Pat Trammell, they were in for a rude awakening. And they sure weren't going to intimidate one Paul Bryant."

About the only negative of that game was Georgia scored on our backup units on the last play of the game.

We didn't play well against Tulane but won 9-0 and dominated Vanderbilt 35-6 in Nashville, setting up a stretch of really difficult contests. Our first game in Tuscaloosa was against North Carolina State and its star quarterback Roman Gabriel, who would go on to have a long and successful NFL career with the Los

Angeles Rams. I'd never seen a quarterback that big. Heck, he was bigger than all of our linemen.

Gabriel was over 6-foot-5 and I'd guess he had to weigh 240 or so, and he was one tough guy to bring down. We shut down the Wolfpack running game but he hit four or five passes in a row and got it to our goal line where he sneaked in for a touchdown. We were behind for the first time all year, 7-0. It would be the last time all year that we would give up a touchdown.

Coach Bryant once said, "My 1961 team played like it was a sin to give up a point." He was right. For the year, we only gave up 1.7 yards per carry. We thought it was sin to give up a first down. Back in those days, you played both ways and could only substitute a couple of players at a time.

I can remember a few games where another player and I would slip down the sidelines and check into a game to keep the other team from scoring when we had our reserves in there and were trying to hold the other team out of the end zone.

We didn't have much trouble keeping Gabriel and the Wolfpack from scoring again that day either. At one time in the second half, I sacked him, and I remember it was like trying to wrestle down a bull at my Excel farm. Man, he was hard to bring down, but we held them to a minus-25 yards rushing that afternoon, and our offense got rolling and we won 25-7.

The next game was against Tennessee, a team that had been the proverbial thorn in Coach Bryant's side. For years and years, the Third Saturday in October was the highlight of the season in Southeastern Conference football, dating back to the classic games when General (Robert) Neyland coached at Tennessee and his teams competed against the Alabama teams of Wade and Thomas.

Neyland was quoted as saying, "You don't know what a player is made of until he plays Alabama." Alabama had been the benchmark for college football, and we were determined to break a Tennessee winning streak that dated back to 1953.

This game was really important for Coach Bryant, because he loved beating Tennessee. As a player, he had played with a broken leg in Knoxville in a 25-0 Crimson Tide victory. But he hadn't had any luck against the Vols as an assistant coach at Vanderbilt or head coach at Kentucky, Texas A&M or Alabama.

Coach Bryant instilled in us on an annual basis, the winner of the Alabama-Tennessee game usually had a chance to win the Southeastern Conference, so we knew we had to be ready to win this one.

As a team we were determined Coach Bryant would enjoy this day.

It was one of those magical autumn afternoons at Legion Field, except for the new upper deck on the east side of the stadium. There apparently was some structural damage and 8,000 fans with tickets weren't allowed in.

The game was our only regular-season televised contest, so I hope those 8,000 who didn't get in found a TV set somewhere to see one of the best defensive performances an Alabama team has ever had.

Actually, we fell behind 3-0 in the first quarter when George Shuford set an SEC record with a 53-yard field goal, something unheard of in 1961. One of our guards, Jimmy Wilson, told Coach Bryant coming off the field, "Don't worry Coach, we are going to beat the hell out of them."

And we did. The Volunteer offense totaled 61 yards for the game and didn't make a first down in the second half. After the Tennessee field goal, we ran the Utah pass to Ray Abruzzese and he broke loose to set up a first and goal. Mike Fracchia scored from the five and the rout was on. Billy Neighbors caused a fumble and recovered it, setting up a TD pass from Pat Trammell to Butch Wilson.

After two Tim Davis field goals, we were up 20-3 at half and in complete control. Touchdown runs by Trammell and Billy Richardson clinched a 34-3 victory, setting off a wild celebration not only in the stands but in the locker room as well.

It was the beginning of a new tradition at Alabama, the smoking of the victory cigars. Our trainer Jim Goostree, who had started his career at Tennessee under General Neyland, was the happiest guy around after we won.

Goose, his buddy and assistant coach Dude Hennessey, and our senior manager Gary White had packed the cigars on the equipment truck, and they pulled them out and gave them to the players. I didn't smoke but I took a puff that day and probably choked when I did. Coach Bryant, who was a cigarette smoker, didn't like cigar smoke but he didn't mind on this Saturday.

That "Victory Cigar" tradition lives on today at Alabama. When the Crimson Tide beats Tennessee, the players still light up cigars in the locker rooms.

I don't know if we had a letdown the next week against Houston but we certainly didn't play well. At half we were ahead 3-0 on a Tim Davis field goal, and finally won 17-0, thanks to a TD pass from Trammell to Brother Oliver and a touchdown run by Mike Fracchia. Our defense started a streak of shutouts that would last until the bowl game.

My old roommate Richard Williamson made one of the biggest plays when he caught a Houston fumble in midair and returned it to the five to set up that Fracchia touchdown. After the win over the Cougars, our defense completely shut down our remaining opponents, Mississippi State (24-0), Richmond (66-0), Georgia Tech (10-0) and Auburn (34-0).

Our series with Georgia Tech reached what turned out to be a controversial – and for football traditionalists – a sad ending in the early 1960s. After we beat them in the 16-15 comeback in Atlanta, Bobby Dodd brought another outstanding team to Legion Field in 1961.

It would be a most memorable weekend, not only because we won 10-0 but No. 1 Texas lost to TCU. We moved up to No. 1 in the country, the first time since the wire services started voting back in the 1930s that an Alabama team had been in the top spot.

The Tech win, though, would turn out to be controversial, and the fallout would last for years. In the third quarter, we had forced Tech to punt and Darwin Holt was blocking on the play. His back was to the receiver and Georgia Tech's

Chick Graning was running down field to cover the punt.

Darwin didn't see Billy Richardson fair catch the ball but Graning did and eased up on the play. Darwin was about six inches shorter than Graning, and when Darwin hit him, his forearm caught him in the jaw, breaking it and knocking out his front teeth.

I always thought, and still do, that there was nothing dirty about the play. We were never taught in any form or fashion to play dirty football, but we were taught to play hard throughout the entire play. I will stand by my conviction that Paul Bryant teams played cleaner football than anyone. From my vantage point on the Graning play, it looked like he just let up and Darwin didn't.

The next morning Furman Bisher, a sportswriter for *The Atlanta Journal-Constitution*, wrote a column attacking our team for playing dirty and Coach Bryant for teaching us to play that way and brutalizing the game. It was an insult to all of us, and fueled a lot of fires that would burn for a long, long time.

Bobby Dodd demanded an apology from Coach Bryant, and he refused to give him one, setting in motion Dodd's maneuver to pull Georgia Tech out of the SEC.

All the outcry from Atlanta seemed to diminish the fact that we had held Tech to under 100 yards in offense and dominated the game. We were the No. 1 team in the nation going into our season finale with Auburn.

The Iron Bowl victory was particularly satisfying because we continued our streak of shutouts against the Tigers, and our offense was just as effective with Billy Richardson scoring a couple of touchdowns.

The win over Auburn clinched the 1961 national championship for the Crimson Tide, proving Coach Bryant correct in his promise to us that if we believed in ourselves and did what was expected of us, we could be champions.

There were a couple of other sidebars to that season. The Rose Bowl, the site of so many legendary Alabama victories, had locked into a contract with the Big Ten and the "Big Five" (the future Pacific-12 Conference) after the Crimson Tide beat Southern California 34-14 in the 1946 game.

By 1961 the contract between the Big Ten and the Rose Bowl had expired and we were under serious consideration to play UCLA. Ohio State had been under consideration but because of academic issues with some of its players, the university had declined a bid.

As players, I don't think we knew very much about it, but it would have been special to play in the Rose Bowl, but ultimately they decided to go with Minnesota of the Big 10 as an at-large team. There's little doubt that a column by Jim Murray about Alabama's segregationist stance played a role in the decision not to let us play there.

Certainly, we didn't think playing in the Sugar Bowl against Arkansas was a consolation prize at all, especially since our defense would have the challenge of trying to slow down one of the greatest players I ever went against, Lance Alworth.

In the days leading up the game, Coach Bryant decided to take us to Biloxi to work out, not wanting the distractions of being in Tuscaloosa or in New Orleans. I don't know if we practiced that hard those days or not, but Billy Neighbors said we didn't.

He told the story about Coach Bryant being infuriated with him because he weighed in at 272 in Biloxi, about 22 pounds more than his regular playing weight. His reward, like for most of us starters, was to play every snap of the game.

Mike Fracchia was the MVP of the game, and set up the only touchdown on a long run to the Arkansas 12. Pat Trammell ran it from there and Tim Davis kicked a field goal to give us a 10-0 lead.

No one had scored on us since the Shuford field goal in the Tennessee game, so a 10-point lead seemed pretty safe, but Frank Broyles had his team ready to play that day and a Razorback field goal cut the lead to 10-3.

In the final minutes of the game, Alworth – who would go on to be a Hall of Fame receiver for the San Diego Chargers and a teammate of mine in Dallas – got behind our secondary. You've got to remember this guy had run a 9.5

100-yard-dash in high school and he could fly. They called him Bambi because he was like a deer on the field.

The Arkansas quarterback George McKinney's pass was too long even for Alworth and we had secured a 10-3 victory, making our 1961 team the first Alabama team ever to win the Sugar Bowl. When people ask me to reflect on the trip to New Orleans, all I can say is that it was a business trip for us. It's not like today where there are lots of parties and festivities and gifts for the players. We had a joint team party, got a watch, got our win and headed back to Tuscaloosa as the undefeated national champions.

Whenever our group has gotten together over the years, I think we have felt like we were the team that returned Alabama to its rightful place in the college football hierarchy, and the common thread we all shared was our relationship with Coach Bryant. I think Coach Schnellenberger was right when he said we weren't the most talented team around but we had a will to win unlike any team he'd ever seen. I like to think we embodied Coach Bryant's preaching to us about a great team having one heartbeat and no individual egos. That really defines the 1961 team.

Not a day goes by that I don't think about Coach Bryant.

Like I mentioned earlier, look at the success stories of members of that team. They would go on to be head coaches, athletic directors, business leaders, doctors, lawyers and educators. It was just a unique group of young men surrounded by a coaching staff with a single purpose and a head coach who was the greatest leader I've ever known.

When I started my lumber business, I took out Coach Bryant's 10 rules for being a successful leader and it still hangs on my wall today.

Reflecting back on the years, I'm proud to have played on a lot of great teams, in championship games, in Super Bowls, but the season I wouldn't trade for any of them is 1961.

TIME OUT: BENNY NELSON

Benny Nelson was a freshman with Lee Roy Jordan in 1959 and went on to have his own stellar career as a halfback for the Crimson from 1961-63. The Huntsville, Alabama, native was an All-SEC running back in 1963.

I was a freshman in Coach Bryant's second class, the same one with Lee Roy Jordan. There was no doubt early on that he was a special player and made the rest of us better. It was like going to war with Superman. You knew you always had a chance with Lee Roy in the game.

We had a freshman game down in Auburn in 1959, and I'll never forget after the game, my dad came up to me and said, "My gosh, that Lee Roy Jordan is some kind of football player."

He had played the entire game, and I promise you he had at least 20 tackles. He was the MVP of the Bluebonnet Bowl in his sophomore year, the star of our national championship in 1961, and the captain of our 1962 team that won the Orange Bowl. I remember there being a buzz in Miami about President John F. Kennedy appearing at our game against Oklahoma.

I'll never forget Coach Bryant telling us in the locker room that President Kennedy was at the game and sitting on the Oklahoma side. He said, "The losing side."

Lee Roy pretty much made that happen. Joe Namath had a great game but Lee Roy had 31 tackles and just completely dominated their offense. It was something that we had been accustomed to seeing every Saturday. It's a shame more games weren't on TV back then so more people could have seen just how great he was.

Off the field, he's always been one of the nicest people ever. On the field, he was a holy terror and a leader. When we were playing Vanderbilt at Legion Field in 1962, they had a linebacker, Sam Sullins, who had been a high school teammate of mine.

It was a close game and we had third-and-short, and Sam stuck his head in our huddle and told Joe Namath to "give Nelson the ball."

The next thing I know Lee Roy is pushing him out of there. There was no doubt I was getting the ball and Sam hoped Lee Roy wasn't blocking him. We made the first down and won the game 17-7.

Lee Roy epitomized what you'd want in a football player. There haven't been many like him.

TIME OUT: JERRY DUNCAN

Jerry Duncan was a freshman in the class that arrived before Lee Roy Jordan's senior season. Originally a running back, Duncan went on to become an all-star offensive lineman and nationally known as the receiver on the tackle-eligible pass.

When I got to Alabama as a freshman in 1962, I didn't know much about anything, including Crimson Tide football. Having grown up in Sparta, North Carolina, I knew about Coach Bryant and that Alabama won the championship in1961.

Well, I learned firsthand about Lee Roy Jordan on my first day of practice. Freshmen weren't eligible back in those days, so we were blocking and tackling dummies for the varsity. We were preparing for the season opener against Georgia and I was a running back my freshman year.

Coach Clem Gryska held up a sheet of paper with the play to run, and I was going to get my first college carry, at least one in practice. I was handed the ball and was running through the line when I just got absolutely waylaid.

About all I remember was seeing stars first, and then blood coming out of my nose. When I was trying to get up, I saw Lee Roy Jordan standing over me. I was thinking, "Man, I would hate to be a Georgia running back if he hits a teammate this hard."

I was also probably wondering what in the world was I doing playing at Alabama.

After practice, trainer Jim Goostree put my nose back together and sent me walking back to Friedman Hall where we lived. I didn't have transportation, and this car comes wheeling up to me. The driver tells me, "Hop in, rookie, and I'll give you a ride to the dorm."

The driver was Lee Roy Jordan. Off the field, Lee Roy was one of the nicest people who ever lived. On the field, he was a one-man wrecking crew.

I played with some great players and against some great players during the next four years at Alabama, but Lee Roy was the best defensive player of them all. He just had that innate skill to make plays, and he'd make them all over the field.

Jerry Duncan interviews me on the sidelines long after our playing days at Alabama.

CHAPTER 6
NAMATH AND THE 1962 SEASON

ertainly, our anticipation in the spring of 1962 was to repeat as national champions, especially since the majority of our team returned and the addition of some outstanding sophomores, most notably Joe Namath.

Through the years there have been a lot of yarns about Joe Willie as a player and a person. All I can say is he was a great teammate and better friend, and certainly one of the most gifted athletes I've ever been around. If not for the debilitating knee injury he suffered his senior year, Joe's legacy would probably even be more pronounced. Even playing with a braced knee and very little mobility, he was still among the elite of all-time.

So, we really felt like we were going to be better in 1962 than we had been in our 1961 run to the championship. Then the unexpected and, in one case, inexplicable happened to our team. In the spring, our star back Mike Fracchia suffered his own knee injury that basically ended his career.

Mike was coming off an MVP performance in the Sugar Bowl and what likely would have been a season when he would have been a candidate to win the Heisman Trophy. He was that good. Of course, back in those days they didn't have the medical ability to structurally repair injuries like the ones Joe and Mike sustained.

While we had a great young back in Benny Nelson, losing Fracchia was a major blow. That paled in comparison with what happened in June. Tom Bible, one of our linemen from Piedmont, went on a fishing and swimming trip near Mobile, and lost his life in a drowning accident.

We had been freshmen together, and he had not only developed into a good player but a good friend. Tom had backed up in Billy Neighbors in 1961 and had moved to a starting tackle position in the spring, but sadly he never had the opportunity to fulfill his dream of starting for the Crimson Tide.

It's never easy for a team to totally comprehend the impact of a death of a teammate, but I know it had to have a lingering effect on us.

Regardless, we prepped for our season opener against Georgia with the attitude that we were going to give everything we had to defend the national title. The opener was going to be at Legion Field in Birmingham, and it would be the first time that Joe Namath would display his unique skills to the Alabama fans and the Georgia football team.

I just wish more games had been televised before his injuries, so the entire football world could have witnessed how gifted a player he was. We beat Georgia 35-0, and Joe only played into the third quarter before Coach Bryant inserted Mal Moore to finish off the Bulldogs. In his two-plus quarters, Joe displayed those talents of his, throwing for three touchdowns, including a 52-yard strike to Richard Williamson the first time we had the football.

Cotton Clark caught the other two, and the rout was on. Little did I know that less than a year later I'd be in a courtroom testifying before a jury that the game wasn't rigged.

After the Georgia victory, we easily won against Tulane in New Orleans 44-6, then struggled to beat Vanderbilt 17-7. Our lackluster performance against the Commodores led to our dropping to second in the polls behind Ohio State. That didn't last long because the Buckeyes lost the next week and we beat Houston to regain the top spot.

When we went to Knoxville on the Third Saturday in October, we were trying to give Coach Bryant his first win there since he played with a broken leg against the Volunteers in 1935. Alabama hadn't enjoyed many pleasant trips to the Smoky Mountains either, having last won in 1954.

There was little doubt we had the better football team, but we were up only 12-7 going into the fourth quarter. Joe Willie had thrown a touchdown pass to Benny Nelson and Tim Davis had kicked a couple of field goals but Tennessee was playing its usual hyped-up game against the Crimson Tide.

Actually, they dominated us in the third quarter and had the momentum going into the fourth, but we lived by the motto about owning the fourth quarter. We did that at Neyland Stadium, outscoring the Vols 15-0 and continuing our unbeaten streak.

We didn't have much trouble in disposing of Tulsa, Mississippi State and Miami, but I have to admit chasing the Hurricanes' elusive quarterback George Mira made that game interesting. We won 36-3, but we had actually trailed 3-0 at halftime.

It was Homecoming in Tuscaloosa, and you can imagine Coach Bryant was none too happy with our performance. Touchdown passes from Joe to Bill Battle and to Cotton Clark got us rolling and we never looked back. We were firmly entrenched as the No. 1 team in the nation, having not lost a game since the Tennessee contest in 1960, and were on our way to Atlanta to Grant Field to play Georgia Tech on November 17.

It would be one of the most frustrating afternoons of my football career. Tech certainly got some revenge on us in 1962, beating us 7-6 in Atlanta.

That game still hurts me to even think about it. There was no question we had the better team, a much better team, actually. I think it was one of the few times I ever saw Coach Bryant actually overestimate an opponent.

In all those previous games against Georgia Tech they had better players, but that just wasn't the case in 1962, especially since we had Namath.

That was before Joe had injured his knee and when he could still run, something that most fans never had the opportunity to see. His passing skills spoke for themselves during his days with the New York Jets.

Anyway, we blew a couple of scoring opportunities early in the game, and Tech went ahead 7-0. We finally scored in the fourth quarter but we just flat missed some assignments on the two-point conversion try that made us miss it. I was fortunate enough to make a play, intercepting a pass that gave us the ball back deep in Tech territory. We missed our chance to win when we turned it over inside the 10 and lost by that 7-6 score. It was a long and disappointing trip home.

As poorly as we had executed throughout the game, we probably got what we deserved. Coach Bryant assumed all responsibility for the loss, which he always did, and gave the credit to winning to Coach Dodd and the Yellow Jacket players.

By the time we were doing our preps for our season finale with Auburn, the players had voted and accepted an opportunity to play Oklahoma in the Orange Bowl on New Year's Day. My four years at Alabama had been a blur and I tell players today, enjoy it, because it will be gone in the proverbial blink of an eye.

First, there was the annual Iron Bowl at Legion Field with Auburn and then there was the NFL draft coming up as well. Before we played the Tigers, the 1962 Heisman Trophy was awarded to Terry Baker from Oregon State, a quarterback that few in our part of the country knew much about.

Certainly, the Heisman wasn't that big a deal back then, and I'm not even sure anyone even told me that I had finished fourth in the balloting behind LSU's Jerry Stovall and Minnesota's Bobby Bell. What was a big deal to me was being chosen as one of the permanent team captains of the 1962 team.

In my opinion, all awards like the Heisman and MVPs and whatever are won by a team, not an individual. It was always about the team as far as I was concerned, but being elected by my teammates to forever be their captain was and still is special to me. Jimmy Sharpe was our other permanent captain, and I know our focus was making sure our 1962 team finished with a win over Auburn.

Really, my only concern was beating Auburn. I guess a lot of people thought that we would have a letdown after the Georgia Tech game, but we had such strong senior leadership that not only did we want to win but we wanted to shut Auburn out for the fourth straight year.

Auburn had been on top of the college football world when Coach Bryant came to Tuscaloosa and it would have been easy for a lot of us to have gone with the winning program, but we believed in Coach Bryant.

When I think of that Auburn game, I have to tell you about how we practiced every day on recovering fumbles, blocking place kicks and blocking punts. We had a special period every day where that's what we did.

It was illegal to advance a recovered fumble, but Coach Bryant drilled us on pushing the ball forward toward a teammate.

If anybody else had been teaching that drill but Coach Bryant, I'd have thought it was a waste of time. I didn't doubt Coach Bryant and by gosh it came to happen in the Auburn game.

On the opening kickoff, Butch Wilson ran it back 92 yards and Namath scored on a 17-yard run. Those were memorable plays, but the one I remember most was when we blocked a punt around the 30-yard line.

As the ball was rolling around, I batted it toward the Auburn goal line. Jimmy Wilson, Richard Williamson, Jimmy Sharpe and Bill Battle all pushed the ball toward the goal untill Bill finally recovered it for a touchdown.

All that practice time for four years on the drill worked to perfection. The final was 38-0, certainly a gratifying conclusion to the regular season. Now I waited to see where I would be selected in the NFL draft.

DRAFTED BY DALLAS

I don't think there was any secret that the Dallas Cowboys were interested in drafting me. Their chief scout Gil Brandt had joined the organization when they opened operations in 1960 and was responsible for finding the talent for Coach Tom Landry. His ability to find players would eventually make Dallas one of the NFL's best franchises.

There were no TV cameras and very little hoopla about the 1962 draft held on Monday, December 3, two days after we had finished the regular season with the shutout win over Auburn at Legion Field.

Gil called me to tell me that Dallas had taken me in the first round, the sixth overall pick. There were only 14 teams in the NFL then and the upstart AFL had eight. I was drafted by the AFL's Boston Patriots, a team where my old teammate Billy Neighbors was starting at guard, but I wanted to play in the NFL and stay in the South.

So my decision to sign with the Cowboys was pretty easy.

I laugh now about agents and negotiating multi-million-dollar contracts. My advisor was Coach Bryant and I told him Dallas was offering me a three-year contract with my first year paying $17,500. He told me to ask them for a car for a signing bonus and that's what I got.

Gil Brandt came to campus and met with Coach Bryant during our preparations for Oklahoma and the Orange Bowl. In his inimitable way, he told Gil that I was going to sign but Coach laid down the law that there would be no more talking to me until after we played Oklahoma.

There wasn't, even though Gil made the trip to Miami and stayed at our team hotel. We were staying at the Sea View Hotel, overlooking the ocean and Biscayne Bay. I went to bed on December 31 never expecting that 1963 would be a most memorable year on and off the football field.

It was legal for local booster clubs to give players gifts back when I played. Most of them gave cars, but I wanted a bull. Here I am getting a Black Angus in 1963.

Bill Battle was a great teammate and an even better friend.

TIME OUT: BILL BATTLE

Before becoming a successful head football coach at Tennessee, a renowned businessman and founder of the Collegiate Licensing Company, and director of athletics at Alabama, Bill Battle was a star end on the Crimson Tide's 1960-62 teams. He was also a teammate and friend of Lee Roy Jordan's.

In the summer of 1959, I was selected to play in the old North-South High School All-Star Game in Tuscaloosa. Before we started practicing, I had never heard of Lee Roy Jordan.

That changed on the first day of practice when I heard this collision. It didn't take me or anyone else there long to learn who made the tackle and who was the best player on the all-star rosters.

When we were freshmen at Alabama, it was pretty obvious that Lee Roy was just a unique player and special person. Obviously, we had a great run during those years, winning the championship in 1961, and we should have repeated in 1962.

The Auburn game in 1962 was a game that we seniors committed ourselves to winning. It was the next game after we had lost the 7-6 game to Georgia Tech, and it would have been easy for us to not to be intense or enthusiastic.

But, we had great senior leadership, and we probably played the best game of the year, winning 38-0. Butch Wilson ran back the opening kickoff and Joe Namath scored on a run. Then, I got a score on blocked punt by Jimmy Wilson. The rules back then didn't allow you to pick up a blocked punt and run it.

So, we had practiced pushing the ball down the field. Lee Roy swatted the football down the field, and then Dan Kearley almost got it. I was lucky enough to fall on it in the end zone for the touchdown.

The next day on Coach Bryant's TV show, he would go on and on about Lee Roy. He would be saying, "There's old Lee Roy making a play, and there's Bill

Battle scoring on the blocked punt. Let me tell you about that Lee Roy Jordan."

All of us who were honored to play with him, either at Alabama or Dallas, could tell you about him. He was that good.

It was legal in those days for local alumni groups to give players who had completed their eligibility a gift. After we won the national championship, it was common for the local groups to give a car to a player.

During the 1962 season, the Excel group would come to Tuscaloosa and take donations outside Denny Stadium to buy Lee Roy a car. They had so few people in Excel, it was the only way to raise any money.

Since Lee Roy was getting a car from the Cowboys, he wanted a bull. Not only did they raise enough money to buy him a registered Angus bull, but they bought him several registered cows to help him start his first ranch. He's probably the only guy during that time to chose cattle over a car!

One of the untold stories on him was at the Senior Bowl. We had just beaten Oklahoma in the Orange Bowl, and I was set to go to be on Bud Wilkinson's staff as a graduate assistant. Coach Bryant had somehow managed to get me on the South team for the Senior Bowl. It would be my last game.

It was big for me, because the Senior Bowl paid the winning team $800 and the losers got $600. For a young guy preparing to go to Oklahoma that money was a big deal. We jumped to a 33-6 lead, but those all-star games had some crazy rules.

If you were ahead by 10 and the other team scored, you had to kick back off to them. Our defense was the on the field the entire fourth quarter. I weighed 205 pounds and was having to play defensive tackle, and going against this big old lineman from Penn State named Chuck Sieminski.

I'd been coached well enough to make some plays, including an interception that I batted up in the air, but we were all worn out in the fourth quarter. Then, Lee Roy proved his grit and greatness.

The North had cut the lead and was threatening to catch us. There was a play that Lee Roy got hit in the mouth, and I looked over and he's on the field.

Blood everywhere. His teeth knocked out.

Our trainer at Alabama, Jim Goostree, was assigned to work for the North team, and he was the first person to reach Lee Roy. Goose was putting gauze in his mouth, trying to stop the bleeding.

Lee Roy just threw the gauze out, and said, "Let's go." There was a sigh of disbelief among our teammates, other than me. They couldn't believe he was staying in the game. Some of them told him to go to the sideline, that it was a meaningless game.

It may have been meaningless to some of them, but it wasn't for Lee Roy. Here's a man, already drafted in the first round by the Cowboys, refusing to leave and refusing for us to lose. The score was 33-27 and the North had first-and-goal on our three. They ran four plays and Lee Roy stopped them all four times, making every tackle on the goal line.

I might have been the happiest guy on the field, because that extra $200 meant a lot to me. For Lee Roy, it was winning the game and making plays for our team. That's Lee Roy Jordan, the ultimate teammate.

We maintained our friendship through the years, and I'd see him when we had reunions of our championship team. In 2012, Lee Roy invited Benny Nelson, Richard Williamson and me to the Alabama-Michigan game in Dallas. We really re-bonded after that.

When I think of all the men who have built and established the tradition of the Crimson Tide, I know one who should be up there with any of them, my friend and teammate Lee Roy Jordan.

CHAPTER 7
THE ORANGE BOWL AND BECOMING A COWBOY

The year 1963 would be one that would forever change my life and no doubt impact the United States in a more profound way with gunshots fired in my new hometown of Dallas.

On January 1, 1963, I was chosen to call the coin toss for Alabama in the stands of the Orange Bowl. The reason was the president of the United States, John F. Kennedy, was going to flip it. And for security measures, the Secret Service requested the president do the coin toss in the stands. It was really a special moment for me, being able to meet and shake hands with President Kennedy.

My impressions of President Kennedy were pretty simple: what a charismatic man, whose wife Jacqueline was just as impressive.

I am not sure if there has ever been a coin toss in the stadium before or since, but the captain from Oklahoma, the referee and I were led into the stands where we walked up to the commander-in-chief. I still have pictures of the event, which I cherish. I also still have the coin that was tossed, and that's certainly among my keepsakes that will forever be a Jordan heirloom.

The game was equally memorable for me, mainly because I closed my college career with a 17-0 victory over the traditional Big-8 power Sooners.

President Kennedy was friends with Oklahoma coach Bud Wilkinson and had named him to a position as spokesman for his physical fitness program. The president had gone by the Oklahoma dressing room prior to the game, but he didn't visit the Alabama locker room. Coach Bryant used it as a motivation for us, but I'm not sure I needed much of a pep talk that day.

I wanted to go out a winner and in a small way erase some of the bitter taste from the loss to Georgia Tech. Oklahoma had a great running back named Joe Don Looney who was quite a character and would go on to have a long and really controversial NFL career. Equally as impressive was the Sooner fullback Jim Grisham, a unanimous All-American.

I got a lot of recognition for having 31 tackles that day as our defense shut down their running game. Really, the credit should go to our coaches and defensive front. Our coaches had noticed one of their linemen tipped off which side the ball was going, and I could spot it pretty easily.

Our linemen kept their center and guards from getting to me, and I pretty much had one of those days that I'll never forget. While Joe Namath was becoming a household word across the country with his passing and running, I was fortunate enough to stop Grisham twice inside the 10-yard line, forcing a couple of fumbles as well.

People always ask me about that game, and I'm glad they remember. I think that's one of the unique aspects about an Alabama player. Our fans never forget. I'd find out the same when I became a Cowboy. The Dallas fans were equally as devoted to their Cowboys.

Gil Brandt was in Miami for the Orange Bowl and then traveled to Mobile to watch me play in the Senior Bowl. I kid Gil that he was pretty eager to sign me to a contract. My main goal was to play in Mobile, knowing it might be the last time I'd play in the state of Alabama.

The Senior Bowl was a crazy game. Our quarterback Glynn Griffing of Ole Miss had the proverbial hot hand, throwing for five touchdowns. We were up 33-6 in the third quarter.

Well, the coach of the North team, the Dallas Cowboys' Tom Landry, pulled his team together and they rallied to score three touchdowns to cut the lead to 33-27. I don't remember our coach Weeb Ewbank of the Colts -- and later Joe Namath's coach with the Jets – giving us a pep talk.

I do remember that our defensive players were determined to make sure we won, and it was really important to me because I wanted to go out a winner in Alabama.

The North had a first-and-goal on the three, and I was in on some tackles on running attempts to keep them out of the end zone. After an incompletion on third down, I helped sack the quarterback and preserve the win.

A few days later, I officially became a Cowboy when Gil flew into Mobile, rented a car and drove to Excel to get me to sign my contract. He brought a basket of food topped by a couple of bottles of whiskey.

My sister Agnes and I greeted him at the car, and told him that we had to hide that liquor because there was no way my parents would let me sign if they knew he had brought alcohol to our house!

With the fifths hidden in the car, I signed a three-year contract for $17,500 for year one, $18,500 for year two and $19,500 for year three. Now, getting my car was quite a story in its own right. I got a Buick Riviera, with a sticker price of $6,200.

Gil was going to bring it to me in Tuscaloosa but lo and behold, he hit a cow on a back road in Mississippi, so it took me a few weeks before I collected my bonus! I'll never forget Gil calling me and asking me if I had insurance on my old car because it would cover the cost. I told him I didn't because I had given it to my sister.

So, I had a wrecked car as my bonus. I did get some cattle, not the one Gil hit! Back in those days, it was legal for local alumni groups to give players a gift after they had completed their eligibility.

The Monroe County Alumni Club wanted to give me a new car, but since I already had one of those, I said I wanted a bull instead. I'm probably the only player of that era who got an Angus bull plus five heifers for my departing gift from college football.

It helped me start my first ranch, and I have to say that was as nice a gift as I could have ever received for playing football.

Regardless, the year 1963 had started off with some memorable on-the-field excitement as well as some off-the-field events that I'd always remember.

Gil Brandt drafted me to be a Cowboy. Tom Landry would be my only head coach in Dallas.

TIME OUT: GIL BRANDT

A graduate of Wisconsin, Gil Brandt served as vice president and chief talent scout for the Dallas Cowboys from 1960-89. Considered one of the most astute evaluators of prospects ever, he still works as a television, radio and print analyst for the NFL. In 1962, he was the man who made Lee Roy Jordan a Dallas Cowboy.

Alabama always had players that were smart and of the highest character. Coach Bryant and his staff not only did a great job of coaching their players, but they did it with the highest quality individuals.

When I was scouting players, it was pretty easy to identify Lee Roy because he was such a competitor. He had great feel for the middle linebacker position, and he fit what we were looking for in Dallas.

His size may have scared away some teams. Coach Jim Goostree, the trainer under Coach Bryant, told me that Lee Roy started the 1962 season at 212 and weighed 199 at the end of the year. One thing he didn't lose was his innate football intelligence and his sixth sense of getting to the football.

He fit the mold of the defense that coach Tom Landry played. We ran a 4-3 Flex defense. Our defensive front kept blockers off the linebackers, and we had some good ones. Our only concern with Lee Roy had nothing to do with his size, but whether he could play in space.

We knew he was great against the run. I had been at the Orange Bowl and knew he had that ability to dominate an opposing team's running game. College teams didn't throw much, so we had no idea how he would be able to cover and tackle receivers in open field. He exceeded our expectations. He was great at the point of attack and great in space. He intercepted a lot of passes in his career. In one game against Cincinnati, he had three interceptions in the first quarter. I think it's still an NFL record.

Lee Roy was a typical Coach Bryant player, just high quality from a high quality family. I'll never forget drafting him and going to Excel to sign him.

I flew into Mobile and went to Delchamps Super Market and bought big wicker basket. And I filled it up with all kind of delicacies and put two bottles of bourbon on top. When I got to the house, Lee Roy and his sister stopped me, telling me there was no way I was going to bring that liquor into their parents' house. Lee Roy and I had to hide the bourbon in the car.

Players didn't make much money back then, and the signing bonuses weren't a lot either. Lee Roy wanted a new car with all the bells and whistles. We got him a Buick Riviera that even had power windows, which was one of the first cars that did.

The Buick dealer had to special order it, and I told Lee Roy that I would drive it to him. So, I go from Dallas to Starkville, Miss., and I'm on my way to Tuscaloosa. About four or five miles out of Starkville, there were three cows in the middle of the road, and I hit one of them and wrecked the car.

Well, there was a guy driving behind me, and he stopped and asked if he could help. I told him to take me to campus and I'd hook up with Johnny Majors, who was an assistant at Mississippi State back then, and he'd get me a place to stay.

It was the day that the Mississippi State basketball team was sneaking out of town to play Loyola in the NCAA Tournament. It was a big deal, because the governor of Mississippi – Ross Barnett – had forbidden any school to play an integrated team, so Babe McCarthy and his team were trying to get out of Starkville.

There were all kind of people at the courthouse, including the sheriff. His name was Johnson, and I told him that I had wrecked Lee Roy Jordan's car when I hit a cow. He said he knew because it was his daddy's cow, and he wanted to know how I was going to pay for it!

I know Lee Roy wasn't too happy about it, either. This was his big bonus and it was a heap back in Mississippi. Eventually, he would collect on his signing bonus from the Cowboys.

Lee Roy only missed a handful of games his whole career. He got hurt in his rookie year and missed a few games in his second. Then, he played 12 straight seasons without missing a game, quite an achievement for any player.

He was an amazing player. He was tough as nails, even though he didn't have the type of size of Dick Butkus or some of the other linebackers. It's a shame that he's not in the pro Hall of Fame, because he was as good or better than any middle linebacker in football. He was one of the greatest players in Dallas Cowboy history and one of the main reasons we had all those great teams in the 1960s and 1970s.

One of the times Lee Roy was hurt was when we played the Cleveland Browns on Sunday, November 24, 1963. It was a time you'd like to forget. President John Kennedy had been assassinated on Friday in Dallas.

Cleveland beat us badly that day, and I'm not sure if Lee Roy would have been able to help us much, although he usually played his best against teams with great running backs and Cleveland had one in Jim Brown. I know one time when we played them Lee Roy had 10 or 11 tackles on Brown and we held him to one of his lowest rushing games ever.

Here's the bottom line. Lee Roy is one of the greatest players in the history of the Dallas Cowboys. He's loyal to the University of the Alabama. He's a special person and his wife Biddie is even more so.

One of the reasons we had great teams in Dallas is we had great people. Just like Alabama. We wanted people with high character. Coach Bryant was particular in wanting smart people with great character.

We passed over a lot of guys in the draft that didn't have character. More than 40 years since retiring, Lee Roy is still a household name in Dallas and in Tuscaloosa. That says a lot about his lasting footprint on two of the most storied football programs in NFL and college football history.

On the sidelines as a Cowboy.

CHAPTER 8
BEATING THE PACKERS; TESTIFYING IN COURT

I n the spring of 1963, I was working out in Tuscaloosa prior to my first professional season in when *The Saturday Evening Post* came out with an article accusing Coach Bryant and former Georgia head coach Wally Butts of fixing the 1962 game. Coach Butts had retired after the 1960 season but had remained on as athletic director, and he was accused of giving Coach Bryant the Georgia game plan during a telephone call.

Mr. Bisher, who was the writer for the Atlanta newspaper, was involved in this accusation, which only ignited even more anger from both Alabama and Georgia fans.

First of all, we beat Georgia 35-0 in that game, and if it had been Coach Bryant's way, we could have beaten them by twice that amount. We were that much better than Georgia. I can assure you that game was not fixed.

The article came out on March 24, 1963, and within days both Coach

Bryant and Coach Butts filed separate lawsuits against Curtis Publishing, Inc., the owners of the magazine. Coach Bryant had already gone on statewide television to denounce the magazine and assure the fans that it was one big lie.

I guess things moved a lot faster in the court system back then, because in early August, I got a registered letter, telling me that I had to testify at the trial in Atlanta. I caught a plane from training camp and flew there to testify on the same day that Charlie Trippi was testifying. Coach Trippi had been on the Georgia staff and had been a legend as a player for the Bulldogs.

Coach Bryant and one of my former teammates Jimmy Sharpe had already been on the witness stand to state the obvious fact that the game had not been fixed. When I was asked to tell the truth, I told the judge that I was going to and I did.

I remember they asked Jimmy and me both about a certain formation that Georgia had used early in the game and how it had caused us troubles, and it had. Our coaches spotted it from the booth, and told us what they were doing. The point was if we had their game plan, we'd have known all about their new formations.

If there was any humor in this whole ordeal, it had to be when Coach Bryant testified. I wasn't there but the story was told a lot by legendary *Birmingham News* sports editor Alf Van Hoose that Coach Bryant was such an imposing witness that when he was looking for his reading glasses and couldn't find them, several jury members pulled theirs out and handed them to him.

Before I testified or got to the Cowboy camp, I played in the first game of the year, the annual College All-Star Game against the Green Bay Packers. Up until 1976, the NFL champion would play against the best college stars at Soldier Field in Chicago. On occasion the college team would be competitive but rarely won.

I was in really good shape, not only because I had been training on a workout plan from the Cowboys; but I had been at Alabama for four years, and I knew what it meant to get in shape. And, when I reported for our practices, I felt like I was in better playing shape than just about anyone there.

We had quite a collection of all-stars, a group of players who would go on to have an immediate and long-lasting impact on the professional level. So, we thought, heck yes, we can play against the Packers.

We had Jerry Stovall, the great back from LSU, who would go on to have an outstanding career as a safety for the St. Louis Cardinals and future Houston Oiler John Baker from Mississippi State. John was known for his knockout punches on defense and as a great blocker as a tight end.

We had one of the best defensive lines imaginable, including two future NFL stars and two of the biggest tackles I'd ever seen, Jim Dunaway from Ole Miss and Buck Buchanan from Grambling. Then there was Bobby Bell at defensive end, Kermit Alexander at safety, Lee Roy Caffey and Danny Brabham at linebacker.

It didn't take me long to realize how much talent we had on defense, and I felt if I could play with these guys against the Green Bay Packers, then I knew I could make it as a linebacker in the NFL.

We had some great guys on offense, too, including Glynn Griffing, who had been the MVP quarterback in the Senior Bowl, and my old Alabama teammate Butch Wilson, who was playing tight end.

I don't know if we shocked the world that early-August night at Soldier Field, but we certainly gave jolt to that legendary Packer team of Vince Lombardi's that featured one of my early idols Bart Starr.

I think that was the first time I ever met Bart, and I shook his hand before the game and told him what an honor it was to be on the field against him. I probably didn't feel quite so generous a few years later when I played against him in a game that I will detail later, the famous or infamous – depending on whose side you were on – "Ice Bowl" of 1967.

Green Bay's backfield featured one of the best fullbacks in football history, Jim Taylor. He was one tough guy, who loved to find linebackers and just punish them by running over them. He had won the NFL rushing championship in

1962, been a perennial All-Pro and was a fearless competitor.

Late in the game, with the Packers needing a yard to sustain a drive, he took a handoff on a third-and-short. I read the play, ran through a hole and dropped him for a loss, something unheard of when it came to Taylor. We had stopped Green Bay and did the nearly impossible, winning 20-17.

I was told the announcers said some awfully nice comments about that particular play, saying it was a picture-perfect tackle. For me it was just instincts, and having been taught the fundamentals of tackling.

Personally, I think I knew then that I could play with anyone.

As a side note, our third-string quarterback was Terry Baker, the Heisman winner from Oregon State. I don't think he took a snap in the game, playing behind Griffing and Wisconsin's Ron VanderKelen.

My August was going to be a whirlwind. Because of the game I was late for practice with the Cowboys. Then I had to get permission from Coach Landry to fly to Atlanta to testify in the Butts trial.

When I finally got to training camp, I had to run a mile under 5:40, which was a requirement of Coach Landry. I never had any trouble completing the run, but a lot of players didn't find it so easy, including our fullback Don Perkins. He was quick and fast but when it came to completing the mile run, Don always struggled, and I think he dreaded that day worse than anyone on the team.

They would test us on just about everything from agility to timing us in the 40-yard dash, and Don would excel in everything but the mile run. I always took pride in being able to complete the mile and I was in peak shape heading into my rookie season, having run a 4.6 40 and being mentally focused on helping the Dallas franchise take the next step toward being relevant.

Legendary Georgia player Charlie Trippi, his wife and I entering the courtroom in Atlanta in August of 1963 to testify at the Bryant-Butts trial.

TIME OUT: BOB LILLY

Bob Lilly was an All-American lineman for TCU before becoming the anchor of the Cowboy defensive front. A member of the Hall of Fame, he has been voted to every all-time NFL team that has been compiled since his retirement in 1974.

I came to the Cowboys in 1961, after becoming the team's first-ever draft pick. Slowly, we began to have some talent, thanks to some pretty good talent scouts, particularly Gil Brandt. Our middle linebacker was Jerry Tubbs, who was born in the same county in Texas and attended the same high school as I did, Breckenridge.

When I was getting ready to start my third season, Jerry's heir apparent showed up in August, 1963, a young man named Lee Roy Jordan from Alabama. All players were leaner back then, because there wasn't much weight lifting. Lee Roy and I used to joke that we were "hay bale strong" because we did our weight lifting on the farm, working the cattle.

Lee Roy was 215 pounds, which may have been a little smaller than other middle linebackers, but we all learned early on that no player was in better condition. And, if we thought he was in shape, that hardly compared with his intensity and desire on the field.

After his first scrimmage, we started calling him "Killer" because he would just literally knock a back to the proverbial next block. I knew instantly this guy was a player, and better yet a friend.

He was always studying, whether it was on the field or the endless hours he spent with Jerry Tubbs off the field asking questions and watching tape.

We had installed the Flex the year before he got there, and Lee Roy learned every aspect of that defense that Tom Landry had created. Lee Roy would define how the defense worked and he would be the best at stopping the running game. Lee Roy devoured the play book and prepared. He had great instinct on the football field, the best instinct of any player I've ever seen. He could recognize the formations and get us into the right play virtually any time the offense lined up.

He would line up behind me, and yell, "Bob." I knew the center was leaning my way. If they were leaning toward our other defensive tackle Jethro Pugh, he'd say "Buzz" to tip off Jethro the ball was coming his way. Lee Roy was like having a coach lined up behind you.

What made him great besides his instincts and intelligence was his strength. He was one of the strongest linebackers in the league. He would take on the biggest offensive linemen and just throw them down.

Lee Roy was fearless. He was on the kicking teams and would race down the field and throw himself into the piles. He was on the field to make plays, and he made them.

When I think about natural-born leaders, I think of Lee Roy Jordan. In practice, he went full blast every play. If someone was loafing, you can bet you'd hear, "Let's go get 'em." It's funny now but our practices were something else after Lee Roy got there. He wanted to punish our offense, tell them they weren't tough and we were never going to be any good until they got tough.

Thanks to his attitude we followed him, and we would intimidate our offense in practice. I guess he learned that from Coach Bryant.

Lee Roy was the quarterback of our defense. He would memorize print-out on opposing teams, and going into a game he would know what they were going to do depending on the down and distance. He'd know what they'd like to do in the first quarter or the fourth quarter. He knew what they'd like to do when they were on a certain hash mark.

Our players learned early on what they had said about him at Alabama: "If they were standing, Lee Roy was going to get them."

Off the field, Lee Roy was the nicest and most cordial young man I'd ever met. On the field, he was a holy terror, one of the best players I ever played with or against. All of sudden, we were believing we were going to be pretty good, and a lot of it had to do with this linebacker from Alabama, Lee Roy Jordan.

Meeting President Kennedy has been one of the highlights of my life. I'm holding
the coin he flipped at the Orange Bowl. I still have it, too!

CHAPTER 9
1963 ... AN UNFORGETTABLE YEAR

By the time I finally put on a Dallas Cowboy uniform for the first time, I had played in the Orange Bowl, Senior Bowl and College Football All-Star Game as well as testifying in a courtroom in Atlanta.

Man, I was ready to play for the Cowboys and learn the defensive system implemented by Tom Landry, truly one of the greatest innovators in the history of the game. I'll talk about Coach Landry in more detail later on, but he was a football genius, not only defensively but offensively as well.

Tom had starred at Texas as a two-way player before joining the New York Giants as a defensive back and later on becoming one of the best defensive coordinators in the NFL. When he arrived in Dallas in 1960 to become the franchise's first head coach, he created the Flex Defense and it was perfect for my game.

My first linebacker coach was Jerry Tubbs, whom I ultimately replaced as the starting middle linebacker in 1965. Jerry was a playing coach, something unheard of today, but he was such a talented player and coach that he quite adequately was able to fill both roles proficiently.

Not only would Jerry be my coach and mentor for 14 years, he became a close friend as well. He had been an All-American at Oklahoma and played on three teams that never lost a game, but before that he had been a star on his high school team in Breckenridge, Texas.

One of his best friends and teammates was Bobby Drake Keith, the old Texas Aggie who had come to Alabama with Coach Bryant and signed me to play for the Crimson Tide. Jerry treated me with so much respect that I couldn't help but have the utmost admiration for him as a man, because everyone knew I had been drafted in the first round to come and be the player who took over running the Dallas defense on the field.

Jerry and I watched film endlessly, picking up everything we could from an opposing team. It's something I had done at Alabama, and being totally prepared was an attribute that Jerry and I shared. I had learned so much from the coaches in Tuscaloosa that I developed an eye for recognizing the small maneuvers by offensive players that might give the defense an advantage.

Jerry Tubbs was the exact same way. We would be watching film, and I'd say, "Jerry, did you see that lineman tip off the play to the left, and we'd re-watch it, until we agreed a player was giving away where the ball was going."

Reading keys to the offense was critical for Jerry and me, because we were calling all the defensive signals. I like to think I was pretty good at calling our defenses at Alabama and at Dallas.

I always looked to see the offensive line splits. Or, if a player's stance was tipping off if he was pulling. If they widened their stance, that meant they were going straight ahead. I'd watch film and pick up little tips from running backs alignments. Jerry and I spent hours searching for the keys to see where the ball was going.

I would take the projector and film home with me every night and watch reels and reels of films of the teams we played, and I think I had a knack to pick up the keys to know what plays they were going to run.

While being totally mentally and physically prepared helped me become a good player, I was gifted with very good quickness. And once the ball was snapped, my first two or three steps got me into position not to be blocked by an offensive tackle or guard and make contact with the runner.

I feel that my other two chief talents were I had good instincts and peripheral vision. Great coaches like Paul Bryant, Tom Landry, Jerry Tubbs or Nick Saban all taught, or in Nick's case still teaches, that you have to use your eyes to make a play. It sounds simple, but for a lot of players it's not that easy.

My first year with the Cowboys wasn't easy. We went 4-10, which makes one wonder by today's standards how long the Dallas management of Tex Shramm (team president and general manager), Gil Brandt (vice president and talent scout) and Tom Landry (head coach) would last in today's football environment.

Let me assure you these three men knew what they were doing in building Dallas into an annual NFL contender, but the first four seasons had yielded records of 0-11-1, 4-9-1, 5-8-1 and 4-10-0. Actually, the patience of the loyal fans in Dallas was remarkable, because I think they could see the caliber of players that were slowly making an impact.

Gil was the first talent evaluator who used a computer and he had more raw data on every prospect than anyone could imagine. Rarely did he miss on a pick either, and with ensuing draft, Dallas was signing elite talent.

Besides having Jerry Tubbs teaching me all the aspects of the defense, I knew my job was going to be a lot easier when I saw how good one of our defensive tackles was, No. 74 Bob Lilly. I had never seen a football player that good, and I still say to this day he's the best I've ever seen.

We would also become lifelong friends off the field as well as playing together in some of the most memorable games in football history.

Early on in the practices, I did everything expected of me and some that rookies probably were scorned for doing things like taking charge when I didn't think players were giving it their all in practice. I just believed in Coach Bryant's teaching that you gave everything you had whether it was on the practice field or in a game, so if I saw a player loafing, I'd call him out.

One day we boarded the team bus to go to the old Cotton Bowl Stadium for a game, and I was stunned that there was no police escort to get us to the game. You can just imagine the traffic and red lights that slowed us down arriving to play a game. When I asked why we didn't have an escort, some of my teammates told me that our management didn't want to pay the money to have one.

I asked the policeman how much would it cost for us to get an escort, and I went to my teammates and raised the money from the players to pay for an escort. I didn't mind telling the management and coaches either that I had been taught by Coach Bryant if you want your players to play in a first-class manner, then you better treat them that way.

Sometime later the Dallas management finally started paying a police escort to help us get to the stadium on time, but I knew from my days at Alabama that if you wanted to be a champion, you better think like one in everything you do.

I liked to think I had been a leader at Alabama because of the way I played and the way I pushed my teammates to do the same; and I wasn't planning on changing in Dallas. And I didn't for 14 years.

There were some really great players on the Dallas team in 1963, especially defensive end George Andrie and cornerback Cornell Green. Two of the outside linebackers were Chuck Howley and Dave Edwards, and I'd go into a lot of football battles with those guys during the next dozen years.

Offensively, the player who really caught my attention – for more reasons that one – was quarterback Don Meredith, known throughout the NFL as "Dandy Don" for his flamboyancy on and off the field. He would become my roommate and I'd be remiss in recounting my career if I didn't devote a lot more time to Don later.

Fullback Don Perkins, tight end Pettus Norman, and receivers Frank Clarke and Billy Howton gave us some weapons, but not enough to really compete with in the tough Eastern Division. Over the next few years, the influx of players on both sides quickly transformed us from pretenders into real contenders.

Entering my first season, I had high expectations for myself and the team. I'd become so accustomed to winning that I didn't realize how talented all the teams were, and each week was a challenge. There were no easy games.

I had my troubles for the first time in my career with an injury. Biddie had traveled from Tuscaloosa for the Washington game, but if we had any expectations of having a fun time after the game, it ended when I got hurt.

I got clipped in the back covering a punt during the game against the Redskins and punctured a kidney, causing me to miss four games late in the season. So my future wife got to play nursemaid during her short trip to Dallas. I couldn't move and had to deal with a lot of bleeding, but the doctors assured me I was going to be okay and the only cure was bed rest. Luckily, I would have only one other injury of any significance during my 14-year career.

In my second season, I dislocated the arch in my foot in the twelfth game of the year. Marvin Knight was our orthopedic doctor. He had spent time in World War II putting people back together, so operating on football players was pretty easy work for him.

He told me he was going to take a bone out from my hip and graft it into my arch, which didn't sound too good to me. But I knew he was a world-class surgeon, so I told him to get it done. Well, when he started to operate, he found I had so many bone chips in my foot that he just took some of those and grafted them into the arch.

One of the few games that I did miss was against the Cleveland Browns on November 24, 1963. I was still recovering from the kidney tear but I was able to drive to the Cowboys' complex for treatments on Friday, November 22.

The facility was only a few miles from downtown Dallas. I was on my way there, listening to the radio, when a special bulletin stopped the world. President John F. Kennedy had been assassinated not far from where I was driving.

All I could think about was not only his tragic passing but about how his wife Jacqueline was doing. My mind drifted back to the first day of 1963 when I had met the president and Mrs. Kennedy in the Orange Bowl at the coin toss of the Alabama-Oklahoma game.

The team was going through its Friday practice, and Don Meredith had just thrown a pass when they all heard sirens blaring. Frank Clarke and Pettus Norman had been talking after running routes and said they hoped something hadn't happened to President Kennedy.

Unfortunately, their fears were indeed reality. The mood was somber among everyone in the Cowboy organization as we awaited word whether the Sunday game against the Browns in Cleveland would be played. Commissioner Pete Rozelle conferred with his old friend and President Kennedy's press secretary Pierre Salinger and decided the game would go on.

I don't think anyone, anywhere felt like playing that weekend, but it was particularly excruciating for the Cowboy players, because everyone was blaming anyone from Dallas for this tragedy. I watched the game on television. The announcers never referred to the city of Dallas. Nor did the radio crews or PA announcer. It was just the Cowboys. Cleveland didn't have much trouble winning the game either. It had been a nightmarish week for the entire country.

As I noted, we finished 4-10 that year, and I started the first seven games – rotating between inside and outside linebacker – before my injury. They didn't keep official tackle statistics but I had three interceptions and caused and recovered a fumble.

The Cowboys were making progress. The fans had embraced the team, but they had been told that this would be a five-to-six year building plan to make the Cowboys really relevant. And, we began to do just that in 1964 and 1965, and the runs for the championships would begin in earnest in 1966.

CHAPTER 10
THE SUMMER OF 1964

I f there was any doubt about the confidence Dallas owner Clint Murchison had in Tom Landry, he ended all speculation when he signed Coach Landry to a 10-year contract in early 1964, despite the fact the team had gone only 13-38-2 in his four seasons.

Mr. Murchison had to make one of the greatest business deals in American history when he became the first major stockholder in the franchise, buying the Cowboys for $600,000 when the league expanded before the 1960 season.

While he was known as a hands-off owner, he was resolute in his belief that Tex Schramm, Gil Brandt and Tom Landry would put together a championship franchise.

It would prove to be a prudent way to do business.

When I got to Dallas in 1963, the team had located its summer training camp to Thousand Oaks, Calif., some 35 miles from Los Angeles. Naturally, it was named for the vast number of oak trees in the area. The practice facility was at Cal Lutheran University in the most beautiful of settings, surrounded by mountains and giant oaks.

There were a number of television shows and movies shot in the area. In the afternoons, I would join Bob Lilly and some other players and jog up the mountain and go to the sets where the hit show *Gunsmoke* was being filmed, starring James Arness.

While we may have been enamored with the Hollywood jet set, some of the stars of the big screen also were starting to take time to come to our practices and become fans of the Dallas Cowboys, most notably the Duke himself, John Wayne.

Along with Elvis Presley, he had been my childhood hero, and I couldn't believe I was not only having the opportunity to meet him, but eventually become a friend of one of the biggest western stars ever.

In 1970 he actually came to Dallas for the premiere of his movie *Chisum* and presented a few of the Cowboys a Winchester rifle like the one he used in the movie. I still have it on display in my office.

Despite our new home away from home during July and August, our daily routine was still focused on football. I still can recite the daily schedule: we would have breakfast at 7:00 a.m. and practice at 9:00 a.m. There were no wasted moments in practice and we would lunch at noon and be back on the practice field at 3:00 p.m.

Dinner would be served at 6:00 p.m. and then it would be team meetings starting at 7:30 p.m. and they often lasted until 10:00 p.m. The rookies always had to entertain the veterans and we had to sing fight songs and alma maters from our respective universities. There were some pretty good laughs on those nights. It was a lot more humorous in 1964 than it had been when I was a rookie.

Another major event in my life occurred June 12, 1964, when Biddie Banks and I got married in Eutaw, Alabama, at her grandmother's home. She remembers a lot more about it than I do! What I do remember most is Dr. Frank

Dr. Frank Rose, then UA President, performed our wedding in 1964.

Rose, then the University of Alabama president and a Methodist minister, performed the ceremony.

Coach Bryant and his wife Mary Harmon had been friends with Biddie's mother. Mary Harmon actually sewed the beads on the veil that Biddie wore during the wedding.

I've got to add this note about marrying Biddie. She's Catholic and since we were not married in the church in 1964, we decided in 1973 to get married in the church in Dallas.

My teammates Bob Lilly, Chuck Howley, Tony Liscio, Roger Staubach and George Andrie were all Catholics. They attended and some participated in the ceremony. Biddie was really happy that we were finally married in the Catholic church.

We had one humorous moment for sure. George Andrie's wife Mary

Lou baked us a wedding cake and my oldest two sons – David and Lee – went around the neighborhood giving out slices of the cake and telling them their parents had gotten married that afternoon. That raised a few eyebrows!

Life was as good as it could get and we really thought we were on the verge of our breakout year when we returned to Dallas.

We thought we had the ability to be a great defensive team, especially since Coach Landry had a veteran group who understood all the parts that made the Flex work. It was really the ideal defense to stop the run, and that was back in the days before the rules changed so much to turn the game more into a pass-happy league.

In a nutshell, here is the best layman way I can describe the Flex. There are eight natural gaps on the front line, and in the 4-3 that most teams were using, the four down linemen were asked to control two gaps each.

In essence, Coach Landry created a picket fence look, with our right end and left tackle lined up in the conventional spot on the line but the left end and right tackle lined up a few feet off the line, giving them better pursuit angles. The linemen had to control only one gap.

The middle linebacker spot now had to control the two gaps on either side of the center. The defense allowed the defensive backs and linebackers to force the play to go where the running backs didn't want to go. It sure helped me make a lot of tackles during my career.

It was a revolutionary defense and created a lot of the motion and spread offenses you see today. It was that hard to move the ball on the Flex.

Jerry was nearing the end of his remarkable career as a linebacker, and I was playing both middle and outside linebacker during the 1964 season. That of course, was before my football injury late in the season.

On paper, the year was disappointing. Dallas went 5-8-1, failing for the fifth straight time to post a break-even or winning record, but there continued to be signs of improvement, particularly in the innovative way the Cowboys were scouting players.

Charlie Waters, Gene Stallings, Roger Staubach and Cliff Harris joined me for this photo opportunity.

I joined Tommy Brooker, Pat Trammell, Coach Bryant, Mike Fracchia and Billy Neighbors to display our championship trophies.

It was a great honor to serve as honorary captain at the 2015 Tennessee game.

Biddie and I have lived a blessed life.

Being inducted in the Dallas "Ring of Honor" is an honor every Cowboy player aspires to achieve. My old teammate and one of the best cornerbacks ever Mel Renfro and team owner Jerry Jones joined me on the field.

I went into the College Hall of Fame in 1983. Jake Reis, Jimmy McDowell and UA President Joab Thomas honored me on the field.

My son David with my mother Cleo, father Walter and me in a picture taken in the late
1960s.

Being a Cowboy was special. I am proud to have been a part of helping Dallas become America's Team.

Family photo taken on Mobile Bay celebrating our 50th wedding anniversary.

The Jordan Family gathered at Bryant-Denny Stadium prior to the 2016 Auburn game.

It is still a thrill to walk on the turf of Bryant-Denny Stadium.

President Kennedy tossed the coin and I called it in the stands before the 1963 Orange Bowl.

I'm combining with one of the best ever, defensive tackle Bob Lilly (74), to make a tackle against the Redskins in a game in the early 1970s.

This is a shot of me on the field during a game in the 1970s.

Biddie and I cutting our wedding cake in 1964.

Tex Schramm had been an executive with the Los Angeles Rams before he took a position with CBS-TV. He was the first person to sell the network on the idea of broadcasting the Olympics, so he was an innovator from the word go.

Gil Brandt had been with him in Los Angeles. He's one sharp man, and he recognized that computers would provide data other teams would not have access to. So, Gil teamed up with an IBM subsidiary in Dallas, Service Bureau Corporation, and developed the first computer program for prospects.

In the 1964 draft, NFL experts didn't think too highly of the selection of a Naval Academy quarterback named Roger Staubach, who had a four-year commitment to the military. Gil didn't care what they thought and he went even farther when he chose Florida A&M sprinter Bob Hayes, the world's fastest man, and a defensive tackle from Elizabeth City State, Jethro Pugh.

Topping it off, he signed free agents who would make an impact. One was an athletic basketball player from Michigan State, Pete Gent. While Gent would become a standout receiver, he would become better known for his novel *North Dallas Forty*.

Another was South Carolina quarterback Dan Reeves, who signed to be a member of our defense as a safety. Due to some injuries in training camp, Dan would move to running back and become a standout for us for the remainder of the 1960s and into the 1970s.

Of course, Roger, Bob and Jethro would become mainstays on our championship teams and become legendary figures on the football field. So, for all of us around the program, I think we could see the master plan of the leadership of the Cowboys paying off.

Another newcomer from the draft was offensive tackle Ralph Neely, who would become a 13-year starter for Dallas and a mainstay on an offense that would become one of the NFL's best.

I always took practice seriously, and to be frank, I just didn't think we were very tough on offense. Defensively, we were developing into the unit that would become known throughout the NFL as the Doomsday Defense, and we would punish the offense in scrimmages.

I don't think some of the offensive players liked it very much, but I didn't think we would ever evolve into a legitimate contender until they toughened up. While Bob Hayes brought game-breaking speed at receiver, giving us a true deep threat for Don Meredith, guys like Dan Reeves and Ralph Neely brought some much needed toughness to the offense and helped to change that mentality.

Our first run for a championship would begin in earnest in 1965, ending with a second place finish in the tough Eastern Conference. Although our record was 7-7, the same as the Giants, we earned the first ever post-season game for Dallas.

Although it was basically a loser's game that no one really to play, the NFL had started a contest between the two teams that finished second in the respective Eastern and Western Divisions. That game was played in the same Orange Bowl Stadium where I had finished my college career. This game wasn't so memorable. We lost to the Baltimore Colts 35-3.

Green Bay beat Cleveland for the NFL Championship in 1965, the last season before the Super Bowl. I think it was significant that we lost two close games to the Browns and a 13-3 contest in Green Bay where we shut down the Packer offense.

I don't believe in moral victories per se, but those close games against the two best teams in the NFL built up our confidence. I really felt that 1966 was going to be the year that we would finally establish the Cowboys as an elite team in the NFL.

While life was good in Dallas, there was one other tragic event for the Jordan Family in 1965, the death of my oldest brother Walter. It was right before I was getting ready to go to summer training camp.

Biddie and I had spent the night with Walter and his wife Mary, and their two children Walter III and Pam. We had actually driven Walter to his night shift at the paper mill. Biddie and I then drove up to Excel to spend the night with my parents. I'll never forget telling Walter that I was worried how he was going to get home from work, and he told me not to worry, that he would catch a ride with one of his co-workers.

Late in the evening, the telephone rang in Excel.

In the 1960s when you got a call late at night in the country, you knew something bad had happened. It was worse than bad in this case. Walter had been killed in a methane explosion at the mill.

Walter had escaped the first blast and had crawled to safety, but he knew there were some of his friends and co-workers trapped, and he risked his life to return to help rescue them. Walter had asthma and according to the medical reports had died of smoke inhalation when he was trying to help his friends.

It was heartbreaking for our entire family, and even after all these years, I still not only miss my brother but feel the pain that my parents and Walter's wife and children had to endure. He died a hero, but I know he wouldn't consider himself that. He was just doing what my parents had taught us, helping others. I can't imagine losing a child, but Walter's death was the second my parents had to live through, with my sister Darlene passing when we were children.

Our family's deep religious convictions are the main reasons they endured the pain of this tragedy. It certainly put football in a proper perspective. I know my family was personally grateful to Rev. Carey and Shirley Robertson for the special attention they paid my parents.

Regardless of the painful loss of Walter, I returned to Dallas and to the grind of playing football, committed to helping the Cowboys become a champion.

TIME OUT: REV. CAREY ROBERTSON

Rev. Cary Robertson and his wife Shirley have been lifelong friends with the Jordan Family. As a young minister, Rev. Robertson moved to Excel. Through the years, he has ministered in nearly 30 nations and across the United States.

In a small community like Excel, the church and the schools are the center points of the community. The church was especially important to the Jordan family, and Lee Roy's father Walter was a leader in the church and the community.

My wife Shirley and I would develop friends across the country, but none have meant more to us than the Jordans. We were a young couple when we moved to Excel and it didn't take us long to build a special bond with the Jordans. We called Lee Roy's mother Aunt Cleo and his dad Uncle Walter.

We were pastoring a church in Bartow, Florida, which is near Lakeland. We resigned from the church. We were told about a vacancy at a church in Excel, Alabama. I talked to Walter Jordan and he invited us to come up for a weekend. I remember driving into Excel for the first time. It was a small farming community.

There was only one blinking red light in town, so that should tell you just how small it was. Monroeville was the closest town, and those folks who didn't farm traveled that seven or so miles there to work in the Vanity Fair Mill.

The church was on a dead-end, dirt road, and I must admit I was a little disappointed when I saw it. Shirley and I didn't have much, and actually needed the offering to have enough money to get back home to Florida.

Uncle Walter and Aunt Cleo invited us to stay at their house, and that started our lifelong friendship with the Jordan family. Even though they had a son who became nationally known for his skills on the football field, there were never any false pretensions among the family. They were just down-to-earth, fine Christian people.

There were only 60 or 70 people in the congregation and when they voted to accept us as their pastors, we readily accepted. Our sons, Phillip and Andy, who were eight and six at the time, moved with us to Excel.

Walter Jordan was a prominent man in the Excel area, owning quite a bit of acreage, and the family was well known throughout the county. We felt honored to become part of their family.

Aunt Cleo was a cook who was simply "out of this world." Everything she cooked was unreal but my personal favorites were her fried chicken and egg custard pie. I can still taste her cooking after all these years.

Of course, all the Jordan family was special. Lee Roy, well you'd never know he was a football star. When he was playing with the Dallas Cowboys, he would come home and always be there at church.

He'd go out in the yard with Phil and Andy and throw the football around with them, just like he was a big kid. Naturally, he was their hero and remained so through the years. I think he inspired them to play the game. Both played in junior college, and Phil went on to play at Evangel College.

After I left Excel, I went to continue my studies at the Baptist Theological Seminary in New Orleans. When Dallas would play the Saints there, we would go to the games and Lee Roy would always give us tickets.

The same was true when I became a chaplain for the United States Navy in Norfolk, Virginia. Every time Dallas came to Washington to play the Redskins, Lee Roy would get us tickets. He'd always invite my boys to the locker room and they got to meet all those great Cowboy stars of that era.

Years later, I found out that Lee Roy was buying us the tickets. I just assumed that they were complimentary, but that was the type of man he is. Even at the height of his popularity, he maintained that quiet, laidback persona.

When Uncle Walter and Aunt Cleo passed way, Lee Roy asked me to come back to Excel to commemorate their lives. While those were extremely sad times, losing such close friends, I was honored and humbled to be called upon to serve as the pastor at their funerals.

Shirley and I still minister today, living in Picayune, Mississippi. We also still talk to Lee Roy. He'll just call to check on us and our family. That's just the type of person he is. I can't imagine a finer group of folks than the Jordan family.

Posed action shot as a Cowboy.

CHAPTER 11
ROOMING WITH DANDY DON MEREDITH

Entering the 1966 season, not many of the national football experts mentioned Dallas when they were selecting favorites to play in the newest event in sports, a post-season game between the champions of the NFL and AFL.

The two competing football leagues had merged into one, and the general feeling was that the defending NFL champion Green Bay Packers would be the favorite to represent the league in the game that had yet to be named the Super Bowl.

When we reached camp that July in Thousand Oaks, I think the prevailing feeling among our coaches and players was this would be the year that Dallas would emerge. I don't remember anyone talking about playing in Los Angeles in this game against the AFL, but I do believe we had our sights on reaching the NFL Championship Game.

I had been captain of the Alabama team my senior year, so when Coach Landry named me the defensive captain, I took the responsibility seriously. This was my fourth year and I think the coaches felt confidence in my abilities to not only lead the defense but to make the right calls from my middle linebacker position.

Also, for the first time, I really felt like we had the explosiveness on offense to match the talent we had on defense. We were on the cusp of having a complete team.

My roommate was the quarterback, Don Meredith, and I could never tell my own story in football without talking about this unique man and legend of the game.

First of all, Don was an extremely gifted football player with one of the strongest arms in NFL history. He was quite a character, popular with his teammates and popular with the women. He grew up in Mount Vernon, Texas, which is about 100 miles east of Dallas.

Don was one of the most highly recruited quarterbacks in Texas, and the coach at Texas A&M at the time, one Paul Bryant, really wanted him to sign with the Aggies. Don allegedly told Coach Bryant, "If you were coaching anywhere else, I'd sign with you, but there aren't any women at Texas A&M and I'm going to SMU."

At SMU, he was not only a star on the football team but so popular on campus that they nicknamed it Southern Meredith University. When the Cowboys joined the NFL in 1961, he teamed with Eddie LeBaron as the original quarterbacks of the franchise.

I tell you how strong his arm was. He and Bob Hayes still hold the NFL record for the longest pass in the air from a quarterback to a receiver, 83 yards. I think the play totaled 95 yards in all after Bob ran it, but you get the point. You hear all the time about how strong a guy's arm is, well that's proof about Don and how far he could sling it.

When I joined the Dallas team in 1963, Don was already a legend around town and in the NFL cities, not only for his immense skills on the field but also for his nocturnal activities. Early on in my career, I guess I had shown Coach Landry just how important football was to me. Having played for Coach Bryant, I had it pretty much ingrained in me that you abided by the rules or you might better check on what time the first bus was headed back to your hometown.

Coach Landry assigned me to be Don's roommate and make sure I kept him on the straight and narrow, apparently something his previous roommates had not been able to do with a whole lot of success. The team would always stay in a hotel the night before the game, whether it was on the road or in Dallas, so I was entrusted not only with preparing for the next day's game but being Don's designated babysitter.

At Alabama, I had been around folks like Richard Williamson and Bill Battle and Mal Moore, players who were as committed to football as I was. Dandy Don was committed to football, but he didn't let it interfere with his nighttime escapades.

To this very day, people come up to me and say, "Man, Lee Roy, I can't believe you made 31 tackles in the Orange Bowl. That had to be your greatest accomplishment in football."

I laugh and say my greatest accomplishment in football was being able to get Don Meredith back to the room in time for bed check . . . . most of the time. I did it for six years, except for one time when we were playing the Giants in New York in 1968. We had already clinched the Eastern Division Championship, but Don was in the fight to win the passing title of the NFL, and he got a bonus if he did so.

I got a cab and we went out to dinner in Manhattan, just the two of us. I thought this is going to be the easiest night ever getting him back to the hotel room, but man was I wrong. Some of the minority owners of the Cowboys were at the same restaurant, and they had asked the stewardesses on the flight from Dallas to New York to join them for a meal.

Don and I had already finished our meals, and I had called a cab to come pick us up, when the owners saw us and waved Don over. Naturally, Don was already entertaining the ladies with his natural gift of gab. He was quite a flirter, and that's an understatement.

I told him, "Come on, Don. The cab is out there, and we are going to miss curfew." He told me he'd be out in a minute, and when he wasn't, I thought the heck with him. I wasn't going to be late for curfew and I really didn't think he'd get in much trouble being there with some of the team owners.

Well, I get back to my room and go to bed and there's no Don Meredith. He wasn't there when I woke up either, but I heard someone trying to fit a key into the door, and I opened it and there was Don. He was quite a sight, and I don't mean a good one either. He'd pulled an all-nighter and was in sad shape!

He showered and tried to drink a lot of coffee, but he wasn't in the best of shape to play football when we left the hotel to play at old Yankee Stadium. And, it showed on the field, too.

He completed only one pass in nine attempts for six yards with an interception. Coach Landry had had enough and benched him. We went on to win the football game, but the passing title passed from Don's hands to Bart Starr's.

On the flight home to Dallas, some of the players pointed out to him that he had lost the passing title. His quip back to us was, "Well, I bet I had a lot more fun last night than I would have had if I had stayed in and won the passing title." Of course, Don went on to become even better known as the colorful commentator for Monday Night Football with Frank Gifford and Howard Cosell. He was just as natural on the air as he was playing quarterback on the football team.

Back in the late 1970s, an old Dallas teammate Pete Gent wrote his novel *North Dallas Forty* loosely based on Don and himself. Don quipped later, "If I'd known Gent was as good as he claimed in that book, I'd have thrown him the ball a lot more."

One of the saddest days for me was when Don passed away from a brain hemorrhage in 2010. That guy was a legendary part of football. Later on, I would room with Roger Staubach. I never had to worry about getting Roger back to the room. His focus on football was just as keen as mine.

When I think about what our team achieved in 1966, I can't help but think about Don Meredith, my roommate, friend and truly a legendary figure in NFL history. And, like so many for the Dallas franchise of that era, it was a season when we were on the brink of football greatness.

We would live on the edge of being the best during Don's last years as a Cowboy, but he was the man who ignited the offense and set in motion a lot of good years for Dallas fans. I think every Dallas Cowboy of that era would agree with me that Don was not only a great football player and leader, but one of the best men any of us had known.

I'm proud to say he called me "Roomie" and saddened that he received so much criticism for our playoff losses. With no disrespect to anyone, I think if he hadn't retired at the age of 31, we would have won a couple of other Super Bowls.

Finally, people who weren't around in those days of football just don't realize that quarterbacks were open targets for defenders and took a beating. Don had so many injuries that it's hard to remember them all, including broken bones, and a crushed ankle. You name it, but he never complained and played his heart out to help the Cowboys become America's Team.

My roommate Don Meredith was not only a great quarterback but quick with a quip. He made me laugh at one of his lines as we boarded the bus before a game.

CHAPTER 12
THE COWBOYS WIN THE EAST

By the time the pre-season games started in 1966, the merger of the two leagues was complete; and Kansas City Chief owner Lamar Hunt had dubbed this NFL-AFL championship game the Super Bowl.

Several rookies had stood out to me in the July drills, particularly offensive guard John Niland out of Iowa and fullback Walter Garrison from Oklahoma State. Gil Brandt had worked his magic again, drafting defensive lineman Willie Townes from Tulsa. He would become a valued member of our Flex Defense.

For the first time ever, Dallas won all five pre-season games, most of them impressively. The most anticipated pre-season game in Cowboy history came when the champion Green Bay Packers came to the Cotton Bowl.

Although pre-season games are indeed exhibition contests, this one had a little bit more intensity, and after we won 21-3, I think there was a prevailing feeling among the players and coaches that this team had the special ingredient needed to make a serious run.

When the 1966 season officially kicked off at the Cotton Bowl in mid-September, the New York Giants were the first team to be stampeded by the best combination of offense and defense in the NFL.

The final score of 52-7 didn't even indicate how badly we had beaten New York. Don Meredith threw five touchdown passes and didn't even play much in the second half. Dan Reeves scored three times on receptions and Bob Hayes got the other two. Both of those guys had over 100 yards receiving.

Minnesota, with its emerging Purple People Eater Defense, played us relatively close the next week before we won 28-17. Fran Tarkenton, the former Georgia quarterback, was the Viking sparkplug, throwing for two touchdowns and proving to be just as elusive as he was when he was running all over the field for the Bulldogs.

While our passing game dominated game one, it was the running of Dan Reeves that highlighted week two. He rushed for 81 yards, caught a pass for 29, and threw a halfback pass for 23 more. The diversity of our offense had started to become the talk of the NFL, and for the first time, Dallas was beginning to gain attention.

After we won 47-14 against the Atlanta Falcons and 56-7 over the Philadelphia Eagles, Dallas was in first place for the first time and the team to beat. Philadelphia, Cleveland and the St. Louis Cardinals were considered the major contenders for the East title, and we had embarrassed each one of them.

In the win over Atlanta, my good friend and linebacker Chuck Howley scored on the longest defensive play of the season, running a fumble back 97 yards for a fourth-quarter touchdown.

It became apparent the next couple of weekends that the divisional race was far from over when we tied the Cardinals and then lost to the Browns in Cleveland, a place that had been a nightmare for the Cowboys throughout the 1960s.

St. Louis – with a win over Cleveland and the tie with the Cowboys – now led us by a game going to the mid-season point of the schedule with Pittsburgh coming to Dallas.

I got into the touchdown scoring act in that game when I intercepted a pass off Pittsburgh Steeler quarterback Ron Smith and returned it 49 yards for a score in the second quarter of our 52-21 rout at the Cotton Bowl.

Actually, we had fallen behind 7-0 in the first quarter and had tied it up on a Dan Reeves run when I had my interception return. While our offense was setting all kind of scoring records, I got to joke with my roomie Don Meredith that I had helped our scoring offense, and he had hurt our scoring defense that day.

One of the Steelers' scores came on an interception return off Don, and another came on a kickoff return by a player named Cannonball Butler. Other than those two plays, the day belonged to the Cowboys. Pittsburgh had only 119 offensive yards while we nearly hit the 500-mark.

Our confidence was growing. We were 5-1-1 at the mid-point of the season, being tied with the Cardinals and a half-game ahead of the Cleveland Browns for the Eastern Division Championship. Then came our trip to Philadelphia.

The old adage about "on any given Sunday" couldn't have been truer than the first Sunday in November. On a blustery, windy day, our defense held the Eagles to five first downs and 88 yards in offense. That mattered in statistics only, because Philadelphia won 24-23 in a game we dominated offensively and defensively.

Unfortunately, major breakdowns in the kicking game proved our undoing. The Eagles' Timmy Brown ran back the second-half kickoff and Aaron Martin did the same on a punt, turning a 17-7 deficit into a Philadelphia lead that the Eagles would never relinquish.

We did turn it around, finishing a three-game road stretch by beating the Washington Redskins and their great quarterback Sonny Jurgenson 31-30 and then the Steelers 20-7. Meredith and our offense was in high gear in D.C. with

Don throwing for more than 400 yards, and he even rushed for a touchdown.

The Redskins did nothing running the ball, netting 23 yards, but Jurgensen had a cannon for an arm and he picked apart our secondary. Four turnovers didn't help us either. We were just glad to win and get back to Dallas to prepare for the first ever Thanksgiving Day game at home.

The NFL was growing in popularity every year, and there was no doubt that television was one of the main reasons. Tex Schramm was the ultimate promoter and started lobbying Pete Rozelle and the Commissioner's Office to add a game on Thanksgiving. Detroit had been hosting a game for years, and the commissioner, seeing the value of having two games, awarded Dallas a game on Thursday, November 24, against the Cleveland Browns.

Cleveland arrived in town with a 7-3 record, a half-game behind us, so the stakes were high, making it the biggest game played up until that time at the Cotton Bowl in Cowboy history. It was one of those games that lived up to its expectations.

The Browns had a 14-13 lead at halftime with our only touchdown coming on a pass from Meredith to Reeves. A pair of third-quarter field goals gave us a 19-14 lead and a fourth-quarter run by Don Perkins gave us a 26-14 victory.

A week later St. Louis came to town with an 8-2-1 record, matching ours, and making this late-season showdown an even bigger game, with the winner likely being the Eastern Division Champion. The whole city of Dallas was abuzz with excitement and rightfully so.

At the end of the day, the Cowboys were winners, 31-17, but it was another game decided in the fourth quarter when we scored a clinching touchdown. An interception by Chuck Howley was a game changer. For the first time, Dallas was set to win a championship.

On the Western side of the league, Green Bay was again steamrolling toward a divisional title, setting up a New Year's Day showdown in Dallas for the NFL title and the right to represent the league in the first Super Bowl. As a team, we knew it would be the ultimate challenge, matching Vince Lombardi and his old guard Packers against Tom Landry and the upstart Cowboys.

Most old-time football fans know that Lombardi and Landry had coached together on the great New York Giant teams of the 1950s. Lombardi had been the offensive coordinator and Landry the defensive genius.

While those two may have differed in personality, both were known for perfection and precision. Green Bay listed its offensive style as hard-nosed, smash-mouth. Entering the game, I knew we'd have to stop their vaunted sweep and play smash-mouth with them. Personally, I liked that and looked forward to the challenge. All of our defenders did.

The weather was ideal for January 1, 1967, with temperatures in the mid-40s and the sky clear. Green Bay was a veteran team with perennial All-Pros like Bart Starr, Jim Taylor, Fuzzy Thurston, Forrest Gregg, Willie Davis, Ray Nitschke, Herb Adderley, Willie Wood, on and on. It was a virtual Hall of Fame lineup.

Conversely, we were one of the youngest teams in the NFL with only Chuck Howley being 30 years old. The rest of us were still in our twenties. I think early on we may have thought we weren't supposed to compete with Green Bay, and it may have looked that way.

The Packers went down the field for a score the first time they possessed the ball. Lombardi had installed some offensive plays we had never seen or prepared for, most noticeably some misdirection runs that worked. Their running back Elijah Pitts and Jim Taylor had some success running, but the play that burned us was a pass to Pitts for the first score.

I take responsibility for it. We had a breakdown in coverage on who was picking him up out of the backfield and Bart hit him on the run for a score. Our bad start became even more nightmarish on the ensuing kickoff when our great corner Mel Renfro fumbled and the Packers' Jim Grabowski scooped it up and ran 18 yards for a touchdown.

If anyone wrote us off early, they were mistaken. Dan Reeves and Don Perkins capped off two first-quarter drives with runs of three and 23 yards, tying the game.

Defensively, we adapted to what Green Bay was doing with the misdirection plays and the Packers' famous running attack was not moving the ball against our Flex Defense. Unfortunately, Bart Star – my old idol – was having one of the best games of his magnificent career.

Green Bay receiver Carroll Dale beat Renfro on a deep pass in the second quarter to give the Packers the lead at 21-14. I really thought we were going into the half tied when Meredith and Hayes combined on a long completion to the Green Bay four, but a sack forced us to use a Danny Villanueva field goal to cut it to 21-17 at half.

Another field goal in the third quarter trimmed the lead to 21-20. The excitement was just beginning.

Deep into the third quarter, Starr again drove the Packers down the field with his passing, culminating the drive with a 16-yard pass to Boyd Dowler. The Green Bay receiver was flipped in the end zone by our safety Mike Gaechter, injuring Dowler's shoulder and almost causing a fight between our safety and the Packer fullback Taylor. Bart Starr intervened and pulled Taylor away, or who knows what would have happened.

The fourth quarter was just as wild. Bob Hayes fielded a punt on our own one and was tackled within the shadows of our goal posts. Green Bay forced us to punt from the end zone, setting up great field position for the Packers.

They couldn't run the ball on us, but we had no answer for Bart. Twice, we had them in long-yardage situations and he completed passes, including a third-and-19 throw from our 28.

Max McGee, who had replaced Dowler, beat our defensive backs for a touchdown that seemed to put the game away. We were down 34-20, and there were no two-point conversions back in those days. An extra point would end it, but Bob Lilly kept us alive when he broke through and blocked the kick.

Maybe we had some renewed energy. All I know was this feeling that we weren't through. While Starr had been brilliant all day on long yard passes, Don

Meredith made his own spectacular play by hitting tight end Frank Clarke on a third-and-20 for 68 yards and a score. Now it was time for our defense to finally stop Starr and we did

After Starr moved the Packers to their 46, we finally made some plays. Dave Edwards and Willie Townes made big stops, and I got Taylor down on third down, forcing a punt. Time was running out when their kicker Don Chandler barely got off a punt and we took over on the Green Bay 47.

In three plays, thanks to a pass interference call on Tom Brown, we were on the Packer two with a first-and-goal. Coach Bryant always thought that games always came down to a play or two, and this one shifted course when our offensive lineman Jim Boeke jumped offsides.

On fourth down, we had one of those breakdowns that just happen. Bob Hayes was lined up in the tight spot where Frank Clarke usually lined up. Green Bay's Dave Robinson recognized it, and rushed Don, forcing a pass that was intercepted by Brown, the same Packer whose interference call had gotten us so close.

We had outgained Green Bay 418-367, had held their running attack to 100 yards and controlled most of the fourth quarter. The Packers made one more big play than us, winning 34-27.

Mark Duncan, then the head of officials for the NFL and a former coach with the San Francisco 49ers, called it the greatest championship game ever, topping the fabled overtime win in 1958 of the Colts over the Giants.

I don't think there was any consolation in our locker room. Even the $6,000 bonus that each of the losing players received didn't ease the hurt.

Tickets to that game cost a whopping $10, which might get you a bottle of water and a hot dog at a game today. The good news was Don Meredith had been chosen as the NFL's MVP and Tom Landry the Coach of the Year. Other than that, the disappointment over losing to Green Bay and missing the chance to play in the first ever Super Bowl soured an otherwise great season.

Regardless, it had been quite an experience, and I think the prevailing feeling among the Cowboy franchise and fans was that there were going to be a lot of championship games in the near future. One would become among the most famous in the history of football just a year later.

I am chasing down a fumbled ball in this photo.

CHAPTER 13
THE 1967 SEASON AND ANOTHER TITLE

While the loss to the Green Bay Packers was difficult on everyone affiliated with our program, I do think it gave us confidence entering what would be another season of change in professional football.

For the first time ever, there would be multiple playoff games. With the addition of the New Orleans Saints, the NFL now had 16 teams, and the Eastern and Western divisions were divided in half with each having two four-team sides.

There were only nine teams in the rival AFL and they would only have one playoff game to reach the Super Bowl.

They named our division the NFL Capitol and paired us with the Philadelphia Eagles, Washington Redskins and the upstart Saints. Based on our 1966 season, we were prohibitive favorites to win the Capitol.

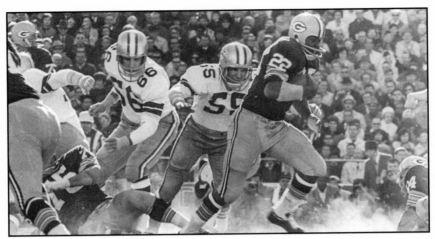

I am tackling Green Bay's Elijah Pitts in the Ice Bowl. It's a day I'd like to forget but can't.

It wouldn't be easy, particularly with the injuries we endured early in the season, especially the ones sustained by Don Meredith. If anyone questioned Don's toughness or will to compete and win, then they weren't around our team during the 1967 season.

Don had his nose busted, cracked two ribs, and re-injured an ankle that was originally crushed years earlier when one of the biggest guys in the NFL, Big Daddy Lipscomb, dove into him in a pile-up. Just when it appeared we would be getting Don healthy, he caught pneumonia and eventually had to go on injured reserve.

Without him, we weren't the explosive offensive team we'd been and we struggled through much of the season. There was one light moment that year, at least now it is. It wasn't too funny when it happened.

We were getting ready to play the Los Angeles Rams coached by George Allen, the former right-hand man to George Halas of the Chicago Bears. Allen was recognized as one of the great defensive minds in football. He was also looking for a motivational edge. Tom Landry was a detail-oriented coach, whose focus on the moment was simply amazing.

Although I wasn't in Cleveland the weekend of the Kennedy assassination, the players who were talked about how Coach Landry was on the chalk board diagramming plays when a security policeman came in to tell the team that Lee Harvey Oswald had been assassinated in Dallas.

Coach Landry never looked away from the board, said thanks, and kept writing. He didn't miss much, so when there was a strange car parked outside our practice, he immediately deployed an employee to go ask the guy what the heck he was doing there.

When our man approached the car, the driver rammed it into gear and sped out of the lot, but the Cowboy employee got the license number and the car belonged to Ram scout Johnny Sanders. This set off a war of words between Tex Schramm and Allen, with the Los Angeles coach in turn alleging that one of our scouts, Bucko Kilroy, was caught spying on a Ram practice from a tree.

Let me assure you of this. Bucko was, in nice terms, a rather big guy and there is no way he could climb a tree, much less escape in time not to be caught. Regardless, the Rams were the best team in the NFL in 1967 during the regular season. Los Angeles quarterback Roman Gabriel, that big old rascal from North Carolina State, was the same one I had managed to wrestle down when we played in college.

Both teams were 2-0 when they came to the Cotton Bowl and the Rams just smashed us 35-13. Gabriel even ran for two scores, so we knew that the 1967 season would have more than just one contender to replace Green Bay as the elite team in the NFL.

We had one of those see-saw type seasons, playing well in spurts and struggling to hang on in others. One of my personal highlights came the first Sunday of November when we played the Atlanta Falcons.

I intercepted a Randy Johnson pass and returned it 33 yards for a touchdown. We won 37-7 that afternoon at the Cotton Bowl, giving us the lead in the Capitol Division. But our stretch run would not be easy.

After a 27-10 victory over the New Orleans Saints, we lost a critical divisional game to the Redskins in Washington. Again, it was Sonny Jurgensen, who caused us nightmares, throwing for four touchdowns in a 27-20 loss for the Cowboys.

While our rout of the St. Louis Cardinals, 46-21, on Thanksgiving gave us some breathing room, the next game was against the legendary Johnny Unitas and the Baltimore Colts. Not only was the game critical to us, but Baltimore was in a fight for its life with the Rams in the Western Division's Coastal Division.

When we got to Baltimore, the Colts were undefeated with two ties, while the Rams had one loss and one tie. Only one of them would make the playoffs.

It was a frustrating day for us, because our defense held the Colt rushing attack to 50 yards, and we led 17-10 entering the fourth quarter, thanks in large part to an interception return for a touchdown by Dave Edwards. Unfortunately, two of those 50 yards came on a last minute TD run by Colt running back Lenny Moore, and Baltimore won 23-17.

In order for us to win our division, we now had to beat the Philadelphia Eagles at home, and we would have to do it without our quarterback Don Meredith. Our backups Craig Morton and Jerry Rhome did an admirable job on a cool, windy afternoon in Dallas, but mainly it was our running attack and our suffocating defense that dominated that day.

Both Dan Reeves and Don Perkins had great games. Dan ran for a touchdown, caught a TD pass, and then threw a halfback pass of 45 yards to Lance Rentzel. That wouldn't be the last time we used that particular play in a clutch situation.

We beat the Eagles 38-17, holding them to 102 yards in offense, and one of their scores came on an interception return. With the victory, the Dallas Cowboys were winners of the Capitol Division of the East and set to host the Cleveland Browns for the right to play the Western Division Champion on its home field on the last day of 1967.

While on the final weekend, we were resting many of our players and losing to San Francisco, the Los Angeles Rams were handing the Colts their only loss of the entire season. Because they were in the same division, Los Angeles won it and earned the right to go to Green Bay to play the Packers.

There was no such rule as the team having the best record having the right to host the playoff games back then. It was pre-determined. Our only focus was getting ready for the Cleveland Browns, the same team that we had opened the season against with a 21-14 victory at Municipal Stadium. Cleveland was never an easy opponent, so we knew we would have to be at our best to beat the Browns at the Cotton Bowl on Christmas Eve 1967.

It was around 60 degrees in Dallas that Sunday afternoon, which hardly compared with what we would face the next weekend. What did bode well for us this day was Don Meredith was completely healed from all his ailments and illnesses and had just a brilliant afternoon, completing 10 of 12 passes for 212 yards, including an 86-yard touchdown strike to Bob Hayes.

Bob had one of the best afternoons in playoff history, catching five passes for 144 yards and returning three punts for 141 more. We jumped to a 24-0 lead and coasted to a 52-14 rout of the Browns, putting us in the championship game for the second straight year against the Green Bay Packers.

Green Bay was getting in the proverbial "old in the tooth syndrome" and most people didn't think the Packers could win against the younger, stronger and quicker Los Angeles Rams on Saturday, December 23. Only a couple of weeks earlier the Rams had beaten Green Bay in the regular season with Roman Gabriel picking apart the Packer defense.

For those who wrote off the Packers, they shouldn't have underestimated the magic of those Green Bay teams. Gabriel and the Ram offense couldn't do anything against the Packer defense this Sunday, and Bart Starr once again proved to be one of the greatest playoff quarterbacks of all-time. Green Bay won 28-7, setting up our rematch. This time the game would be played at Lambeau Field in Green Bay on the last day of 1967.

It would turn out to be the coldest game in football history, the "Ice Bowl."

In the locker room before a game in 1967.

CHAPTER 14
THE ICE BOWL

There may have been another football game played in colder weather, but I'd have a hard time believing it. If I could in any way adequately tell you how cold it was at Lambeau Field I would. I can tell you on Sunday morning, I answered the wake-up call at 7:30 a.m. from the front desk at the Appleton Holiday Inn.

I'll never forget the lady, almost in a cheerful tone, say, "Good morning. It's minus 17 degrees outside in Green Bay, Wisconsin." Nor will I forget New Year's Eve, 1967. Historians often say the NFL Championship Game between the Dallas Cowboys and Green Bay Packers is one of the greatest games ever played.

Really, it was two teams trying to survive the most brutal conditions imaginable. I think the frigid weather better suited Green Bay because they were at least used to playing in the cold, while most of our players just weren't.

Having grown up in south Alabama, and then living in Tuscaloosa and Dallas, a chilly day to me was when the thermometer got below 32 degrees. I think we'd all have been ecstatic if the temperature had even been above zero. When our star receiver Bob Hayes walked into the room for the team breakfast, his eyes were bigger than the coffee cup saucers and I thought, "He's scared to death of playing in this cold."

Bob was a south Florida guy whose whole game was predicated on his unmatched speed. Maybe he thought the icy field would limit his skills, but I really believed he had a fear of playing in the cold.

In retrospect, he was smarter than the rest of us. He kept his hands in his pants most of the game to try to keep them warm. After the game, most of us were dealing with frostbite on our fingers and that would have a lingering effect on us for the rest of our lives. I can tell you that when it gets around freezing now, my fingers start aching like I'm getting frostbite in them all over again. That's no joke.

People often ask if we had brought extra clothing to Green Bay, but we hadn't. Actually, when we flew out of Dallas on Saturday morning, the temperature in Green Bay was in the mid to high 30s and all indications were that it would be the same on Sunday.

The only extra clothing we brought were some brown gloves. You know, the kind that you wear to work in the yard. They hardly helped. Adding to the misery of the day, the field started freezing up when they took the tarpaulins off. We had practiced at Lambeau Stadium on Saturday, and the field was in excellent shape.

I didn't hear the conversation, but the legendary Green Bay coach Vince Lombardi supposedly told some of our administrative and coaching staff that the Packers had a state-of-the-art heating system created by General Electric that would keep the field from freezing.

Green Bay had been one of the first facilities to use such a heating system, but it malfunctioned on Saturday night. Some of our players thought someone had intentionally shut them off to gain an advantage and the whole episode became known as "Lombardi's Folly." Whether that's true or not is left for debate among the players and fans from the respective teams.

There was no question that we had the quicker and faster team, and we really thought we had a much better team than Green Bay. The year before when we lost on the final seconds to them in Dallas, I think they may have had a mental edge because they had been in so many big games and really that had been the first one for the Cowboy franchise.

In the aftermath of the 34-27 loss in the '66 championship game, I think we all felt we had the better team. Going to Green Bay in 1967, we were an extremely confident team.

The impact of just how cold it really was hit home when we found out they had cancelled the pre-game show because band members' wood instruments froze and those with brass instruments literally had their horns stick to their lips. Several members were transported to the hospital, suffering from hypothermia.

The game even started a little late because some of the whistles from the officials froze. The referee for the game was Norm Schachter and his whistle froze to his lips. The officials quickly got plastic whistles to call the game. One of our vice presidents, Gil Brandt, the talent scout who had drafted and signed me, often talks about the coffee in the press box literally freezing.

The old New York Giant player and announcer Frank Gifford was calling the game, and said on the air, "During the next break, I'm going to take a bite out of my coffee."

There had been some talk before the game that it might be postponed, and I've been told that Commissioner Pete Rozelle actually considered it, before making the declaration that the game must go on.

He was out on the West Coast, watching the Raiders play their way into Super Bowl II. If he'd been in Green Bay, he'd have had a realistic perspective of what the weather was really like. The game went on, with the average temperature being a minus 15 and the wind chill factor a minus 48.

Early on everything seemed to go against us. It was almost a repeat of the game in Dallas a year earlier. Bart Starr hit two touchdown passes to Boyd Dowler and we were behind 14-0 in the second quarter when our defense started playing up to our own high expectations. The Packers' Herb Adderley had intercepted a Don Meredith pass and Green Bay was actually in position to put the game away, but our defensive end George Andrie sacked Bart to take them out of field goal range.

Later in the second quarter, Willie Townes sacked Bart, forcing a fumble that Andrie picked up and ran into the end zone for a touchdown. Now the game was on, especially after the Packers' Willie Wood fumbled a punt and we recovered it deep in Green Bay territory.

Our kicker, Danny Villaneuva, kicked a field goal right before halftime and it was 14-10 at the break. I guess we were all ready to get to the locker room and try to thaw out, but I don't remember getting much relief from the cold.

I know one thing that Green Bay's defense had picked up on: Bob Hayes would bury his hands in his pants on plays except when he was the primary target, really making us play with 10 against 11. Despite Bob's ineffectiveness, the Cowboys drove to the Packer 17 in the third quarter, but Meredith was sacked and lost a fumble. Another Dallas drive ended when Villaneuva missed a field goal.

If nothing else, our offense had gained confidence and we finally went ahead in the fourth quarter on a halfback pass from Dan Reeves to Lance Rentzel. It was not only a great play call but perfectly executed.

Dan, who had played quarterback at South Carolina, was running to his left when he stopped and hit a wide open Rentzel for a 50-yard score.

Green Bay's offense really hadn't done much since early in the game, but I can assure you none of us underestimated Bart Starr.

The field was so frozen by the time the Packers took over the final time that we were really having a difficult time keeping our footing. We had several critical slip-downs when Green Bay marched to our goal line. When Green Bay called its final timeout, the ball was on the one-yard line.

According to weather documents, the temperature had dropped to a minus 21 with the wind chill factor at a minus 70. I know Bart has told the story many times over the years that he told Lombardi on the sidelines that he could sneak it in.

While Starr was meeting with Lombardi, our defensive linemen were stomping their cleats into the ice, trying to chop up this iceberg where we were trying to play football. Bob Lilly came over to me and said, "Lee Roy, we need to call time out and get some ice picks and chop up the ground." He wasn't joking. Most people figured they'd try to pass on third down, because an incompletion would give them one more play to decide whether to try to tie it or win it.

When I played, the fullback was an integral part of the offensive schemes with most teams, especially the Packers. Chuck Mercein was their fullback in 1967, having replaced their legendary star Jim Taylor.

My assignment was to stop Mercein, whether he tried to run it or be a receiver, so I was concentrating on making sure I stopped him from scoring. Naturally, if I had known they were going to sneak it, I would have moved up closer to the line of scrimmage.

Jethro Pugh was our left defensive tackle and that's who Green Bay decided to attack. We all thought on defense that the Packer guard Jerry Kramer jumped the count, and I think if you watch video of the play, you can see him move a fraction before the snap.

Regardless, it helped Kramer and Green Bay center Ken Bowman get leverage on Jethro and clear him out for Bart to sneak it into the end zone. There was no flag and Green Bay won 21-17.

Our locker room was pretty silent, a group of players disappointed in the outcome while also trying to assess their physical damage from the cold. My only surprise was that none of us had to be taken to the hospital.

The flight back to Dallas was one of silence. It was an airplane filled with disappointed players and coaches who felt the better team had not won.

When I'm asked about the game now, I really wonder if it should have been played. People comment how great it was. As I said earlier, it really was two teams just trying to survive. I have to wonder if Pete Rozelle had postponed it until the field was in reasonable playing condition what the outcome would have been. That's something we will never know.

And, let me assure you I'm taking nothing away from the Packers because they had to play in the same conditions. It was just indescribable.

Later on, Rozelle would tell people that as long as he was the commissioner the Super Bowl would be played only in warm environments because of what had transpired in Green Bay on the final day of 1967. That gave us little consolation.

TIME OUT: WALT GARRISON

Walt Garrison was a fullback for the Dallas Cowboys from 1966-74 and one of Lee Roy Jordan's roommates during those glory days of America's Team. He had starred at Oklahoma State before joining the Cowboys and was well known on the professional rodeo circuit as well.

I knew a lot about Lee Roy Jordan before he ever knew who I was. I was a freshman linebacker at Oklahoma State in 1962, the year after Alabama had won the national championship when Lee Roy was the star of the team.

Our new coach was Phil Cutchin, who had been an assistant on the Alabama staff under Coach Paul "Bear" Bryant. He had been with Coach Bryant at Kentucky and Texas A&M as well, so our new system was identical to what he had learned under Bryant.

That was still in the time where you played both ways, and I was a fullback-linebacker. All we did in learning Coach Cutchin's system was watch tapes of Alabama, and it was pretty easy to notice Lee Roy. Not many people remember that he was a dang good center, but there was no doubt he was born to play linebacker.

When I got to Dallas in 1966, I learned a lot of football from not only the Cowboy coaching staff but from the veteran players. It wasn't by design or expected, but the veteran players took a special interest in teaching the rookies everything they knew.

I was the back-up fullback to Don Perkins my first two years, and he did everything to make me better. I asked him one day, "Why are you being so nice, because I'm trying to take your job?" His reply: "All I want is for us to go to the Super Bowl, and if you beat me out and help us get there, then that's great."

I think that was the prevailing attitude among the players, and certainly that was the way Lee Roy led the defense. I wanted to learn everything I could about defenses to help make me be a better fullback.

Lee Roy taught me a lot of little things, like watching where certain defenders lined up, so I'd be in position to make the correct blocks.

He also helped me to become a better player in practice. We had a drill called "Blitz." And, the one guy you hated to have to try to block was Lee Roy Jordan. He wasn't that big but he had quickness and instincts galore. He also had the most wicked forearm that I ever got hit with, in practice or in a game.

Lee Roy wasn't known as "Killer" for nothing. Before I got to Dallas, a lot of the players said he was the reason the offense got tough, and I believe it. The other players fed off his intensity, whether in practice or in the games.

One thing we had in Dallas that was special was the leaders of the team didn't let bad blood linger around among the players. There's no team in the history of football that doesn't have squabbles among the players. You can't go out there and knock each other around in practice on hot August days without some hard feelings creeping up.

The quarterbacks and middle linebackers are recognized as the leaders of the team, and when I got to Dallas, the players would go out together after practice. If there were problems, Don Meredith and Lee Roy Jordan would take care of them.

I think that's why we never really had any race problems either. It didn't matter what color somebody was. We were a team and we bonded as one.

There was more than one time when the team wasn't playing up to our expectations that Lee Roy would tell the coaches, in a nice way, to leave the room, and he would take center stage and tell us what was expected of the team.

Lee Roy always gave 100 percent in practice and in the games, and it was easy to feed off his energy and his will to win. You just don't see many players who are so committed to their jobs.

In my opinion, the reason Lee Roy was such a great leader was because of Coach Bryant. He saw that Lee Roy was the type of player who gave all his guts on every play and expected the same of his teammates. I think Coach Bryant also saw that Lee Roy had the courage to speak up and make sure if a player wasn't living up to his expectations, he sure didn't mind telling the player to step it up.

I'm sure Lee Roy had innate leadership abilities, but I think Coach Bryant refined them when he was playing at Alabama, and it carried on to his 14 years as a great linebacker in the NFL.

As most people know, I was a rodeo performer, dating back to my high school days. Most of the guys had off-season jobs, but I was the only one who competed on the rodeo circuit!

Coach Tom Landry wasn't too keen on that idea. He came to me and told me if I ever got hurt, then I wasn't going to get paid to play football. Can you imagine that today? One of the events in rodeo is bulldogging, where you ride your horse and then wrestle a steer to the ground. One day I placed second in a bulldogging event, and lo and behold, Coach Landry's at the rodeo.

He tells me, "Garrison, that doesn't look too tough."

I said, "It's not as tough as blocking Lee Roy in the blitz drills!"

Lee Roy worked in business real estate, but he had grown up around horses and cattle and knew all about them.

A group of players came up to ride horses with me, and I admit that none of them had a chance of being much of a real cowboy, including Lee Roy!

My only regret for Lee Roy is that he's never been voted into the Pro Hall of Fame. What a player. I don't know what that deal is all about. He was the general of one of the greatest defenses of all time, and his records speak for themselves. He should be in for just being the leader he was, but he always had the most tackles and was among the leading pass interceptors for linebackers in football.

Before the 2015 Alabama-Tennessee game in Tuscaloosa, I got to visit with Lee Roy and Biddie Jordan. My friendships with them date back to our early days with the Dallas Cowboys. They are two wonderful people.

I guess you can say that we grew up together back in those days. We were young people involved with a great franchise, and we grew old together.

On road games as well as home games, I had the unique opportunity to become friends with some great football players who were just great people. Over the years, I realized those bonds of friendships that we developed during the early years of "America's Team" only strengthened as time went by.

Lee Roy was a player that I always looked up to, not just as a magnificent linebacker but because he's just one of the best people that you will ever meet.

As a young radio guy who had to interview players in the pre- and post-game, I can tell you that Lee Roy was just heartbroken during all those tough losses to Green Bay and Cleveland in the playoffs. With that being said, he was a person who I could interview who would be honest, contain his emotions and be professional in every manner. That's not easy when you lose a championship game. It takes a lot of class and dignity, and Lee Roy has tons of that.

I'll never forget the Ice Bowl in Green Bay. I didn't go to the sidelines until the game was just about over, and the field was just a blanket of ice. During the game, we had closed the window in our radio booth window to try to minimize the cold, but it didn't do much good.

At one point, I think right before half, I got up and wandered around the press box. I went into the CBS box. Frank Gifford, Jack Buck and Pat Summerall were in there doing the broadcast.

Gifford put a cup of coffee in the window. And, the coffee was frozen. That's not just some story. That happened and tells you just how cold it was that day.

In the locker room, George Andrie, the great defensive lineman, had all kinds of frostbite problems. All the players were just bitterly cold and bitterly disappointed because they felt, as I did, the best team hadn't won. It was a miserable day, and I guess we all felt the pain of that loss.

The first Super Bowl loss was bad, too. Bob Lilly threw his helmet 40 yards after the loss, and that's the game that Lee Roy used as the rallying cry to get the team ready for the 1971 season.

When you put the win over Miami in Super Bowl VI in perspective, you have to think about the job the defense did in completely shutting down the Dolphin running game. No one had done it that season, and they sure didn't the next two seasons.

That was certainly a day that no one affiliated with the Dallas Cowboys will ever forget. I really can't remember any game that Lee Roy didn't play well, and I was there for just about every game he played for the Cowboys. That pretty much tells you about his career. Lee Roy was as good as any linebacker in football. Period.

CHAPTER 15
NEXT YEAR'S CHAMPIONS

A fter our heartbreaking losses in the championship games to Green Bay, I think everyone assumed that it was only a matter of time before the Dallas Cowboys played and won the Super Bowl. I wish I could say that was the case, because if we had taken care of business the Cowboys would have competed with the Packers and Pittsburgh Steelers for the title of "Team of the Decade" for the 1960s and 1970s.

Unfortunately, we got labelled with a lot of not-so-kind nicknames like the "Chokeboys" and "Next Year's Champion" and "Paper Champions." It was doggone frustrating for the players and coaches because we pretty much owned the regular season in 1968 and 1969, finishing with 12-2 and 11-2-1 records, and winning the division by five games in '68 and by four in '69.

The 1968 season would be marred early on when Dan Reeves tore some ligaments in his right knee and was lost for the season. He would never be the same all-purpose back again, which certainly hurt us, not only for losing a great player but one of those players who was a born leader. Dan would come back and play for four more seasons, while also being elevated to a coaching position by Tom Landry.

Then came the playoff games that generated those unkind nicknames and some that were probably a lot worse. During the 1968 season, our offense finished first in the NFL and defensively we were second only to Baltimore, the team that everyone assumed would play us in Dallas for the right to go to Super Bowl III.

Baltimore would indeed go to the Orange Bowl to face my old teammate Joe Namath and the New York Jets. I think anyone who cares about the history of football knows what happened in that Super Bowl. Joe did his thing and forever solidified his name in football history when he led the Jets to the biggest upset in Super Bowl history.

We never got our chance to play Baltimore, much less the Jets, thanks to our playoff loss to Cleveland. In the regular season, we beat the Browns 28-7 at the Cotton Bowl in a game that we controlled most of the afternoon. So, we were prohibitive favorites to win the playoff game and return home to host the NFL Championship Game.

On a cold, wet afternoon in Cleveland, our dreams of being champions turned into a nightmare. Our offense that had been so efficient during the regular season had one of those days that you'd like to forget but never can. The final score was 31-20, but we turned the football over four or five times, and our final touchdown came in the final minute, making it look closer than it was.

Chuck Howley ran a fumble back for our other touchdown, which I guess illustrates the futility of our whole trip to Ohio. Don Meredith had his worst afternoon of the year. Quarterbacks usually get credit when everything falls your way, and they are the goats when they don't.

On one pass play, Don hit a wide-open Lance Rentzel but the ball ricocheted off his hands and was returned for a touchdown. Such was our afternoon in Cleveland. There was one unforgettable, poignant moment off the field that was aired on CBS television.

Knowing that game was out of reach, Tex Schramm made his way to the sidelines and embraced a crying Don Meredith near our bench. I guess they were both trying to console each other for a loss that just was hard to explain.

When we got on the airplane to fly back to Dallas, no one noticed that Don had slipped off before it took off. He caught a flight to New York to meet with Frank Gifford, the New York Giant star who had become a television personality. Although it would be a few months before Don officially announced his retirement and would begin a new one as a broadcaster, there is little doubt that the loss in Cleveland and subsequent trip to New York marked the end of his career.

I had lost a roommate and the Cowboys had lost a quarterback and offensive leader, but television would soon be blessed with an analyst who brought insight with his down-home humor.

With no disrespect to Don's successor, Craig Morton, I always thought that if Don had come back we would probably have won it all in 1969 and certainly in 1970. In 1969, after we won the division, we earned a spot in the playoffs for the fourth consecutive year. Except this time, we would be hosting Cleveland and not having to travel to the banks of Lake Erie and play at Municipal Stadium where we had never had much luck.

Being in the Cotton Bowl didn't help much either that year, because Cleveland just whipped us good, 38-14. About the only bright spot for Dallas fans that day was the play of rookie quarterback Roger Staubach in some mop-up duty late in the game.

As a side note to the end of the 1968 and 1969 seasons, the NFL still had that runner-up bowl game in Miami between the two teams that lost in the championship game. Vince Lombardi had labeled it the "Losers Bowl" and everybody agreed with him. Thank goodness, they ended that miserable experience after we got beat in the final one after the 1969 season.   We lost to the Rams 31-0. The only reason I know the score is I had to look it up. What I didn't have to look up was the feeling that no one wanted to be there, including the fans. If they said they had 20,000 in attendance, that would be a stretch.

The good news for me personally was I was selected to the All-NFL team and chosen to play in the Pro Bowl for the third straight year. The games were played in the Los Angeles Coliseum, and while it wasn't close to being like a regular-season or playoff game, it had a more competitive feeling than the "Loser Bowl."

Thinking back on those playoff losses in the late 1960s, some of our players may have begun to believe we were chokers and next year may never come. I know it was taking a toll on all of us, including Coach Landry.

I'd like to talk about Coach Landry, the man and the coach. How can anyone talk about the history of the Cowboys or the NFL without talking about my coach? Tom Landry was as fine a Christian man as I ever knew. He never tried to push his beliefs onto others, but he was quick to quote from the Bible.

His favorite verse was John 3:16, and it became pretty much ingrained in my psyche. I can still hear him reciting Bible verses, particularly that one. Family was also extremely important to him, and it was important to him that his players also were devoted to their families.

We would have family days at our practice facilities on Saturdays before the games. By 1969, Biddie and I had two of our three sons, David and Lee, and I can still see them crawling around with the children of the other players.

People may have dwelled on the losses in the playoffs, just like the players did, but it was a special time in my life. Being a member of this great organization, building lifetime bonds with my teammates, and playing the role as father as well made those years so unforgettable for all the good that happened to me.

And, I really believe the overall atmosphere that we enjoyed was because of Tom Landry. Coach Landry was a smart, smart man, who had earned his engineering degree from the University of Texas, and he used it to his fullest advantage in being a teacher on the football field. He methodically and meticulously studied the game from an engineering standpoint and pretty much refined proper steps that each position player should take on each play.

He was like Coach Bryant in that he wanted quality people around him and people who believed in his system and were willing to give everything they had to execute the intricacies of the system.

I'm sure when he was playing for the New York Giants as a defensive back and then becoming their defensive coordinator, he started developing what would become one of the most innovative defenses in NFL history, the Flex.

The Flex ideally suited my skills. During my years in Dallas, we didn't have many of those great running backs gain a lot of yards against us. In the Flex, if every player carried out his assignment, it didn't leave any running lane for the running backs. I was lucky enough to play with a lot of great players who were not only good athletes but extremely intelligent as well.

While Coach Landry's defense was one of the most innovative in football, so were his offenses. Because of him, the Cowboys were way ahead of the team we were competing against in so many areas, utilizing motion with our backs and receivers, creating mismatches, calling plays from the press box. You name it. We were doing it.

People have asked me why our offensive linemen would stand up before going into their stances back in those days. It was a Tom Landry innovation at its best. With the linemen standing up, the opposing middle linebacker wasn't able to see the alignments of the backs, making it difficult to call the defensive play.

I think because of the high energy that we played with on both sides of the ball, the Dallas Cowboys were becoming a team that fans all across the country were drawn to watch, whether on television or when we were on the road.

I'd grown to appreciate the Alabama fans during my playing days because wherever we traveled, there were Alabama fans there. It was the same in Dallas. Typically, you didn't see any opposing fans in the NFL. That changed with the Cowboys. Wherever we played, there would be Cowboys fans everywhere. I attribute that to the legacy that Tom Landry was building in Dallas.

Because of our entire organization, we were winning a lot of games, except for the big one. You know you have to win a lot of big games to ever make it to the championship, but the failure to grab the ring became a source of frustration for everyone affiliated with our franchise.

I always thought Coach Landry was one of most brilliant people I've ever known. If he had a weakness as a coach, he didn't have that ability that Coach Bryant had of motivating every player to play at his dead level best, and I think that hurt us in some of our losses. We had better players, a better team, in those games we lost. We just didn't play up to our abilities when it mattered most.

Maybe all those close calls helped set the stage for our championship runs in the 1970s, but there would be one more setback on the field before we could forever end the people calling us chokers.

TIME OUT: DAN REEVES

Dan Reeves played running back for the Dallas Cowboys from 1965-72 before becoming one of the NFL's best coaches, leading both Denver and Atlanta to the Super Bowl. As a coach and a player, he participated in a record nine Super Bowls.

If there was one player who epitomized what you wanted in a teammate and helped make the brand of the Dallas Cowboys what it is today, it was Lee Roy Jordan. He was exactly what you wanted as the leader of your defense, because no one out-prepared him.

He was so dedicated to making himself better every day, and the team better every day, that he made all of his teammates sit back and take mental notes. He made us all better because of the way he would work overtime, his dedication to the team and the loyalty he had to all of us.

I had played quarterback at the University of South Carolina. After I went undrafted after the 1964 season, I signed as a free agent with the Dallas Cowboys as a safety. So early on, I got to watch Lee Roy run the Flex Defense.

It was a perfect defense for him. He could spot the little nuances of the offenses and just flow to the hole to make the tackle. I would learn just how hard he could tackle first hand.

I'd only played halfback once in my life, as a high school freshman. We had a player forget his shoes on a road trip, and the coach put me in. I was all excited because I was going to get to run the ball. It never happened, because the other backs always got the call.

So, in my rookie year in Dallas, there were some injuries to our halfbacks, and Coach Landry moved me to the offense to see if I could play there.

I'm thinking, "Well, now I'll finally get my chance to run the ball from the halfback position." I was all excited, until I got hit for the first time by Lee Roy.

We were having a scrimmage, the offense vs. the defense. Coach Landry set it up so that whoever won the scrimmage would get a steak dinner and the losers would get hot dogs or baloney or something like that.

Don Meredith called a trap play up the middle. On my first carry, I just got smashed. I was getting up from the ground, looking at my facemask that was shattered. Thankfully, I couldn't see my lip because it was busted up worse than the facemask.

I'm thinking to myself, man if he plays like this in scrimmages, I'd hate to go against him in a real game. After the scrimmage, I told him that, and he said, "Dan, if my grandmother put on a helmet and ran the ball for the other team, I would have to tackle her!"

When I'm asked how did Dallas' defense become known as the Doomsday Defense, I'd say it had to be having to play against Lee Roy Jordan in a scrimmage. It was doomsday.

Lee Roy would become one of my best friends, a lifetime friend. When I first signed with the Cowboys, Biddie helped me find a place in in the same apartment complex where the Jordans lived. When my wife Pam and I bought our first house in Dallas, we lived about 50 yards from from the Jordans.

Off the field, he is one of the best people I've ever known. On the field, he was the best middle linebacker I've ever seen. He was sideline to sideline on every play for 14 years in the NFL. He called all the defensive signals.

When the team was down, he would grab his teammates by the shoulder pads and lead us back on the field the next week with the expectation that we were not going to lose.

When we did lose all of those championship games, he was the glue that kept us together. After Baltimore beat us on a last-second field goal in Super Bowl V – a game we just gave away – it was Lee Roy who got us together and told us that we were going to outwork every team and win it all the next year, and we did.

When I'm driving down the highway to this day and see the number 55 on a milepost or any type of sign, I think of Lee Roy Jordan. I can't put into words what a great player he was or what a great man and friend he is.

We were a close team on and off the field. Even after retiring, we continued to see each other. Here I am with Don Meredith, Dan Reeves, Coach Landry and Mike Ditka.

CHAPTER 16
NFC CHAMPS AND SUPER BOWL BOUND

I n Dallas, the 1970 season may be remembered as the one that we finally won the NFC and played our way into the Super Bowl. For the team, it was a season that certainly wasn't the most harmonious one, on or off the field.

Craig Morton and Roger Staubach were battling for the starting quarterback job, and there were times when Coach Landry would alternate them on every other play. There was growing discontent among the players that one of them needed to be named the starter.

That quarterback controversy proved to be problematic throughout the season. Then, there was the situation where Coach Landry benched receiver Bob Hayes for his lackadaisical play and not playing up to the Cowboy standards.

Our offense was frankly running on fumes. Our great running back Calvin Hill injured a knee in mid-season and was lost for the season. Then came the suspension of our other wide receiver Lance Rentzel.

He was married to the actress Joey Heatherton, who divorced him after he got in trouble and was dismissed from the team for an off-the-field incident. Lance had more than 1,000 yards receiving in 1968 and led the NFL in TD receptions in 1969. He was having his best year yet in 1970, so his suspension from the team really hurt our passing attack.

On an early November night in the Cotton Bowl, we took on the St. Louis Cardinals in a key game for the NFC East Championship. It had to be one of the most embarrassing performances by a Dallas team during my 14-year career.

Our only offensive highlights were the tough running of Walt Garrison and a long pass reception by a third-year receiver from Alabama, Dennis Homan. Our defense was just as bad, giving up four rushing touchdowns. We usually didn't give up that many in a year, much less a game.

So, after that pathetic performance, we were in third place in our division with a 5-4 record, two full games behind the Cardinals and one behind the Giants. Our prospects for winning a division for the fifth straight year were made even bleaker because we had already lost twice to St. Louis and split with the Giants.

The next weekend we traveled to Washington to play the Redskins, a team that had lost its coach Vince Lombardi to cancer before the year started. They weren't having a very good year, and we won easily 45-20.

Our Thanksgiving game, the final one played at the Cotton Bowl, was against our old nemesis, the Green Bay Packers. Bart Starr was in the twilight of his Hall of Fame career. Running back Donny Anderson along with receiver Carroll Dale were a couple of the remaining players from the Ice Bowl.

It was in the sixties in Dallas on Thanksgiving, and neither team did much offensively. Coach Landry had decided on Craig Morton as the quarterback, so we finally had some stability there. Our running attack had evolved into an efficient one with the emergence of rookie running back Duane Thomas and the blocking and running of Garrison.

I'll talk more about Duane later, but I'd be remiss if I didn't say a lot of the coaches and players thought he had an attitude that didn't conform with the way we did business in Dallas. Regardless, we finally beat the Packers 16-3, with 13 of our points coming in the fourth quarter, including the only touchdown of the day, an end-around run by Hayes.

The Cardinals tied a game and then lost to the Giants, so all of a sudden, the Dallas Cowboys were back in the title chase, but we knew we had to win the rest of our games. I'm proud to say that our defense played on a level that not many teams had ever reached.

We shut out the Redskins 34-0 and then went to Cleveland to play another old nemesis, the Browns. In the first quarter, we forced a punt that Bob Hayes fielded on our 10. When Bob tried to escape tacklers, he ended up in the end zone and was tackled for a safety.

It seemed like the game was going to end up 2-0. Cleveland barely gained 100 yards on us, and interceptions by Dave Edwards and Charlie Waters gave our offense some field position. But we weren't having much success moving the ball.

Finally, the running of Thomas and Garrison got us close enough for Mike Clark to kick two second-half field goals. The final score was 6-2. We'd have a similar game in a few weeks in the playoff.

We closed the regular season with Bob Hayes reminding everyone that he still had game-changing speed. He scored four touchdowns on passes from Morton and we beat Houston 52-10. With St. Louis losing again and the Giants going down, we somehow got our act together, took care of business and won the NFC East.

In the Houston win, I had one of four interceptions thrown by the Oilers. We also had seven sacks and held them just over 100 yards to go with our best offensive day of the year. We netted some 550 yards.

Entering the playoffs, we again were a confident team, but we knew from our previous experiences that these games took on a higher level of intensity. With all the distractions during the season behind us, I thought we were destined to finally reach the Super Bowl and win it.

The Detroit Lions came to the Cotton Bowl with an 11-3 record and on a five-game winning streak. The NFC now had three divisions and the Lions were the wildcard team, finishing behind the Vikings in the division.

Detroit had one of the best defenses in the NFL, and it was the Lions that helped us get into the playoffs, thanks to their win over the Cardinals a few weeks earlier. We knew it was going to be a tough, defensive game. I liked that. It was an old fashioned struggle, just like our games with the Browns. There would be no touchdowns and not a lot of offensive action by either team. Mike Clark kicked a field goal in the first quarter, and I really thought that would be the only score until we got two more in the fourth quarter.

Two of our great defensive linemen – George Andrie and Jethro Pugh – chased Detroit quarterback Greg Landry in the end zone and tackled him for a safety, marking the end of the scoring. The 5-0 Cowboy win is still the lowest -scoring playoff game in Dallas history.

We held Detroit to six or seven first downs and about 130 yards in offense. One thing was evident, though: We knew our defense would have to carry us to the Super Bowl.

All the other teams left alive in the playoffs were really good on defense, and it was pretty obvious that we weren't going against any more teams with weaknesses like the Oilers.

While we were beating the Lions, the San Francisco 49ers had earned the other spot in the championship game with a 17-14 upset over the Minnesota Vikings in Minneapolis. In preparing for the trip to San Francisco, we knew our defense would have to play at its highest level yet.

The 49ers were the highest-scoring team in the league, thanks to the passing of John Brodie and the receiving of Gene Washington. It would be a challenge, but our defense loved challenges. We were determined to slow down Brodie and his high-flying passing attack.

It didn't take long for John to hit Washington for a long pass inside our 10, but we held them and forced a field goal after Brodie missed running back Ken Willard, who was running wide open in the end zone. Our offense was having no luck moving the ball but we did get a Clark field goal to tie it at the half.

In the third quarter, our defense really took control of the game. Dave Edwards sacked Brodie, pushing them back inside the 20, and on the next play, I intercepted a Brodie pass and ran it back to the 13-yard line. Every time I saw John after that play, he'd kid me about making me a hero that day on his lousy pass.

I don't know if it was a lousy pass or not. I do know on the next play, Duane Thomas ran for a touchdown, breaking several tackles on the way to put us ahead 10-3. On the ensuing drive, Brodie moved the 49ers into our territory but Mel Renfro picked him off to set up a long drive by the Cowboys.

Thomas had a great game that day, rushing for over 100 yards. So did Walt Garrison, who made a clutch run on a screen pass to keep the drive alive and scored a touchdown on a pass from Morton from five yards out. We were up 17-3 and hung on to win 17-10.

I don't remember any wild celebration that you would expect from a team that had earned its way into the Super Bowl. For me, it was just a relief that we had accomplished one goal, but there was the main one to go.

Our opponent was going to be the Baltimore Colts, the old NFL team that had agreed to switch to the AFC when the two leagues officially merged. The venerable Johnny Unitas was still the quarterback for Baltimore and his long touchdown pass to Ray Perkins was the key play in the Colts' victory over the Oakland Raiders to get them in the Super Bowl.

The game was scheduled for the Orange Bowl, where we had played in the Loser's Bowl the previous two years and where I had one of my most memorable games as a college player. Despite all our problems in 1970, we entered practices for Super Bowl V as a two-point favorite.

For the first time all year, we had two full weeks before our next game. Actually, it wasn't an off-week at all. Coach Landry and the staff worked us like a normal game week. I always felt that we were prepared to play a game on Sunday, January 10. We peaked a week too early.

Baltimore had been to the Super Bowl two years earlier, and although they had new coaches, their players were prepared for what to expect that week in Miami. That was hardly the case for the Cowboys.

We weren't sequestered in a hotel. There were fans, media and family everywhere. We'd get phone calls at all hours from people wanting tickets, and there were distractions with the endless requests for interviews.

No one was prepared for the week, players or coaches, and we had a bad week of practice. That's not an excuse for the way we played, but that's just how our week went. I do remember vividly taking Bob Lilly and some of my defensive teammates to dinner at Joe Namath's restaurant outside Miami.

Joe had forever become a symbol of Super Bowl greatness when he led the Jets to a win over the Colts two years earlier. Naturally, Joe was very familiar with all the tendencies of the Colts and he shared with us his thoughts on Baltimore. He didn't think the Colts could move the ball on us, and I think we all felt the same way.

The game became known as the "Blooper Bowl," "Blunder Bowl" and "Stupor Bowl." It was a football comedy of errors and reinforced that image of the Cowboys being the "Chokeboys."

To be blunt about it: We should have won the football game.

In the first quarter Chuck Howley intercepted a Unitas pass, the first of 11 turnovers in the game. We didn't take advantage of that one, but we did get a pair of Mike Clark field goals a little later to go up 6-0.

Then, there came a pass play for a Baltimore touchdown that in our minds shouldn't have been one. Unitas was not the quarterback that he'd been in his heyday, and his passes hardly had the zing they once did.

In the second quarter, he overthrew a pass for his receiver Eddie Hinton, who tipped the ball into the air. At that time the rules stated that another offensive player couldn't officially catch the ball unless a defender touched it.

It was ruled that after the pass bounced off Hinton's hands that our Mel Renfro tipped it into the hands of Baltimore tight end John Mackey, who ran 75 yards for a touchdown. No one on our defense thought that Mel had tipped it. Mel sure didn't.

There were no replays then to say otherwise and Baltimore's touchdown stood. If there was any consolation, they muffed the extra point, leaving the score at 6-6.

In the second quarter, I made one of the most memorable tackles in my career, and probably one I wished I hadn't made. On a third-down play, Unitas was flushed out of the pocket and was running up field when I saw him heading toward me. If I ever made one of those so-called picture perfect tackles, it was on Johnny.

The ball went flying and Unitas was slow to get up. His ribs were injured, and after one more series, he was through for the day, having completed just 3-for-9, including that tipped touchdown. I don't think Baltimore would have ever moved the ball on us if Unitas had remained in the game.

We did recover the Unitas fumble and scored a few plays later on a pass from Morton to Thomas to go up 13-6. Unitas came back for his final series, but he fluttered a pass that Renfro intercepted and we really had a chance to put them away before half. We didn't score then, but we did have a great goal-line stand to end the first half.

Quarterback Earl Morrall, who had played poorly and was considered the goat of Super Bowl III when the Colts lost to the Jets, came off the bench and drove Baltimore to our two-yard line. They never gained another yard. On fourth down, instead of trying a field goal, the Colts went for it and didn't score. We went to the dressing room up 13-6.

It had been a bizarre half and the second one would be just as crazy. After the Colts fumbled the second-half kickoff, Morton drove us to inside the one-yard line. Then another controversial play happened. Unfortunately, the ruling again went Baltimore's way.

Thomas took a handoff from Morton and appeared ready to score when the Colts' Mike Curtis knocked the ball loose. When they un-piled the players, our center Dave Manders got up and handed the ball to the referee. We assumed it was our ball, but the officials ruled otherwise.

There is little doubt that any score at that time would have probably given us the Super Bowl. Instead, it revived the Colts. There would be more penalties and more turnovers to come. Morrall did have some success moving the Colts, but Chuck Howley ended another drive with his second interception.

Then there was a fluke play that is hard to describe. Baltimore was trying a flea-flicker pass, but Jethro Pugh read it and forced their back Sam Havrilak to throw the ball toward Mackey instead of lateraling it back to Morrall. In desperation, Havrilak heaved the ball. The football went over Mackey's head into the hands of their receiver Hinton.

He was off to the races for a touchdown when Cornell Green ran him down and knocked the ball loose around the 10-yard line. The ball rolled toward the end zone and there was a mad scramble. No one could recover the bouncing ball, and it went out of the end zone for a touchback.

That was our last break. An interception return to our three-yard line set up Baltimore's tying touchdown in the fourth quarter. Late in the quarter, our defense forced a punt and we took over near midfield, needing just a field goal to win.

We were penalized ten times for more than 130 yards that day, but none hurt worse than the last one. A holding penalty, which was 15 yards from the point of the foul then, pushed us back to our own 40. On the next play, a tipped ball was intercepted by Curtis who ran it close enough for the winning field goal by Jim O'Brien.

It was a sick, sick feeling. That was the game that Bob Lilly must have set a world record when he picked up a helmet and just heaved it about 40 yards across the field. Defensively, we had created seven turnovers and for the only time in Super Bowl history, a player on the losing team was the MVP. Chuck

Howley got that honor. But he was like the rest of us, it didn't mean much considering the final outcome.

I vowed to the coaches and my teammates that we were going to win it all the next year. I believed it. It wouldn't be easy, but most good things that happen come with the price of hard work and never giving up. That would happen to the 1971 Dallas Cowboys.

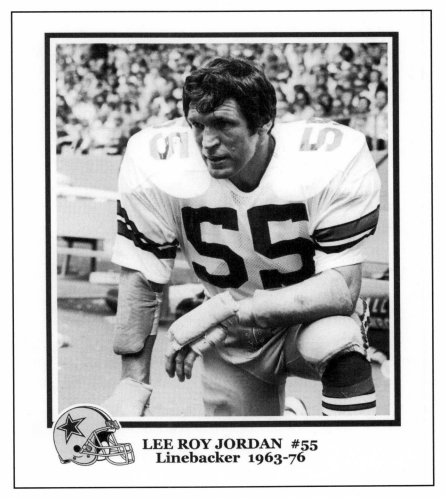

LEE ROY JORDAN #55
Linebacker 1963-76

Collectible trading card during my playing days.

TIME OUT: ROGER STAUBACH

Roger Staubach, the 1963 Heisman Trophy-winning quarterback at the Naval Academy, would become one of the greatest quarterbacks in NFL history during his career with the Cowboys. He served as one of the team captains alongside Lee Roy Jordan, as well as being a roommate.

After I finished at the Naval Academy, my first obligation was to fulfill my military duties. I had been drafted by the Dallas Cowboys, knowing that it would be four years before I would be able to join the team full-time.

I knew about Lee Roy Jordan because of his remarkable career at Alabama and his early days with the Cowboys. He really caught my attention when I watched the 1967 Ice Bowl game with the Packers.

Naturally, I was pulling for Dallas to win the NFL and go to the Super Bowl, and despite the loss, I was amazed at how good this linebacker was. When I finally made the team and subsequently became the Cowboy quarterback, my admiration for Lee Roy only grew.

I like to think I was a student of the game. Lee Roy certainly was, and I think there was a mutual respect between us; so much that we became roommates during his final seasons at Dallas.

Coach Landry was not only a fantastic coach and human being, he was truly one of the innovators in the game, both offensively and defensively. He installed motions and linemen standing up on the offensive line where the defense couldn't see where our running backs were lined up. He mastered creating mismatches, and our offense was always near the top of the NFL.

The "Doomsday Defense" became the standard in the NFL during the 1960s and 1970s. It was not only because we had so many superb players, but because we had Lee Roy Jordan leading them. He was the leader of the defense, make no mistake about it.

At practice, he made the offense better because he had the defense fired up like every session was a real game. They were relentless.

I really think the turning point in my career came in the 1971 season when I was named the starting quarterback midway during the season. I know I drove Coach Landry crazy because I liked to run the ball, and he was definitely a drop-back quarterback man. Craig Morton was our other quarterback, and he had a strong arm and probably fit what Coach Landry liked to do better than I did.

Through the first seven games, Craig and I had alternated, including a game against Detroit when we swapped out after each play. Finally, after we lost to New Orleans in old Tulane Stadium, the coaches made a decision to go with one quarterback, and I was the choice.

I think the team would have done just as well if Coach Landry had picked Craig, because up until that point we had a lot of division on the team. We really needed the stability of one quarterback. Quarterbacks are universally recognized as the leaders of the offense, but defensive leadership can vary.

Usually, it is the middle linebacker but in our case, there was no doubt it was Lee Roy. He was an inspirer, and he let the rest of the defense know that we were not going to be denied in our quest to win the Super Bowl.

Having a defense led by Lee Roy helped me to take risks that I probably would have never taken with a lesser group. I knew that even if I made a mistake, the defense would bond together and make a stop.

We went through the rest of the 1971 season undefeated and finally brought home the Super Bowl championship to Dallas when we beat Miami 24-3 in New Orleans.

I really can't express the happiness and in some way the relief we felt winning that game, because there had been so many close calls before we finally accomplished the mission of being the best in football.

I was fortunate enough to be picked by the media as the MVP, but it was really the defense and our running game that carried the day. Most of the credit has to go to Lee Roy. He had spent hours studying the Dolphin offense preparing for the biggest game of the year.

He just had that unique ability to find something that an opposing offense would do and put our defense in a position to stop them.

Miami had the best running attack in pro football, but they didn't gain 100 yards against our defense that afternoon. A lot of that had to do with all of our great players like Bob Lilly, Jethro Pugh, Chuck Howley, Dave Edwards, Cornell Green and Mel Renfro, but most of it had to do with Lee Roy making the right calls to get us in a position to stop Miami.

As happy as I was about winning, I was just as thrilled for men like Lee Roy who had built this franchise into the nationally recognized brand it became. They were the ones who built a tradition of excellence and made the Dallas Cowboys a name recognized everywhere you go.

The only thing I can't understand is why Lee Roy Jordan is not in the Hall of Fame. Oh my gosh, I just don't even understand that. He was the heart and soul of some of the greatest teams in football history. He's one of the best football players ever to play the game, enough said.

CHAPTER 17
THE GOAL: WIN THE SUPER BOWL OR BUST

After we had lost Super Bowl V and had returned to Dallas, our whole team was despondent. I think that sinking feeling that the Cowboys would never win the big game became a prevailing sentiment among the Cowboy players, particularly all of us who had suffered through all those excruciating losses.

A lot of us were on the back half of our careers, so we knew we weren't only battling self-doubts but the old clock as well. Maybe I had one advantage that most of our guys didn't have. I had played for Coach Bryant, and the word "quit" just wasn't part of his vocabulary. He instilled that into his players who endured playing for him.

I reached back to that philosophy he had ingrained in me, and I felt it was my responsibility to be the leader he would expect me to be during the 1971 season. Coach Bryant had drilled it into me that to be a leader, I had to give it everything I had in every drill of every practice, and make the other players dig down into their souls and give every ounce of ability they had to do a little bit better every day.

I made it my personal mission to lead Dallas back to the Super Bowl, and this time we were going to win. Even when we faced some disappointing moments during the regular season, I never backed down in my personal resolve to help this team become a champion. There would be some rocky roads along the way to the Super Bowl.

Our offense had a new face, Lance Alworth, whose speed was a perfect complement to Bob Hayes, making our wide receivers perhaps the fastest in football history. Lance had been a perennial All-Pro for the Chargers since his days at Arkansas. I'd never forgotten how good he was from having played against him in the Sugar Bowl a decade earlier.

We opened the 1971 season with two road games, winning in a wild shootout in Buffalo, 49-37 and then a much easier 42-7 game in Philadelphia.

Buffalo featured O.J. Simpson, who netted only 25 yards rushing on our defense. I intercepted a pass, as did Chuck Howley and Charlie Waters. Despite our picks, Buffalo passed for almost 400 yards on us to keep it close. That was frustrating.

The next week's game against Philadelphia was much easier and one that I'll always remember in a positive light. Officially, we held the Eagle running attack to 32 yards and intercepted Eagle quarterbacks seven times, including six off starter Pete Liske.

Herb Adderley, who had joined us the year before after starring for 10 years for Green Bay, had three interceptions. Bob Lilly got into the scoring act by running a fumble back for a touchdown. It was a record day for me as well. The official scorer credited me with 21 tackles, which still stands as a Dallas Cowboy record.

Philadelphia's only score came on a return of a missed field goal, so we felt a whole lot better about our defense than we had after the first game.

There was excitement building because we were scheduled to leave the Cotton Bowl and move into our new facility, Texas Stadium in Irving. It was a state-of-the-art stadium for that time period, and while we had enjoyed a whole bunch of successful Sundays in the old stadium, we were eager to move.

Well, it didn't happen until October, because Texas Stadium wasn't ready yet, so we stayed in the Cotton Bowl for two games, including a Monday night 20-13 win over the Giants.

If Super Bowl V was a comedy of errors, our last game in the Cotton Bowl was a close second. There were 11 turnovers, including five lost fumbles by the Cowboys. Coach Landry continued to shuffle quarterbacks, and there was a feeling that we just couldn't build enough continuity in a game to be as efficient as we needed to be.

The next week proved we could play worse. We traveled to New Orleans to play the New Orleans Saints in Tulane Stadium for the fourth time since they had joined the league in 1967. I had never lost there, including my trips with the Alabama teams to play Tulane and Arkansas in the Sugar Bowl.

It was also the site of Super Bowl VI, so we were hoping this would be a positive omen for the Cowboys.

I had always liked playing in New Orleans because there were always a lot of my friends from Alabama who would drive over, including the Jordan family's minister from Excel, the Reverend Carey Robertson and his family.

We were favored by a bunch, but we were down 17-0 at the half. While our offense had been ineffective, our defense hadn't been much better. Their rookie quarterback, Archie Manning, ran for a couple of touchdowns, including one that clinched a 24-14 victory for the Saints.

Then, we moved into Texas Stadium, playing New England. It was our best performance of the first half of the season. We led 34-0 at the end of three quarters, with some late scores by the Patriots making it look closer than it was. In the first game in Irving, Dallas had won 44-21.

If we thought that win had set us sailing on the right course, we were wrong. Next up, we faced the Chicago Bears.

We looked about the same as we had in New Orleans and lost 23-19. To be blunt about it, as a team we had not shown up to play against the Bears, and that didn't set well with me.

After we had lost on Halloween Day at Chicago, our record dropped to 4-3, and we were behind the Washington Redskins in the NFC East race. To put it mildly I didn't think some of the players were giving their best effort. I'll leave it at that.

When we got back to Dallas, I told Coach Landry that I was calling a players' meeting and no coach was invited to attend. I got up and read the team the riot act. I basically told them that from this day on until we won the Super Bowl, every player on the team better commit himself to making the Cowboys champions.

Back in those days, a lot of players still had jobs during the season to make some extra money, and I told them to quit their other jobs and be football players. I probably said a lot else that wouldn't be printable.

After I spoke, Bob Lilly got up and reiterated what I had said. Then a few other players made similar remarks. From that day until the season ended, there was a new focus, a new resolve among the players to accomplish our mission.

Coach Landry made an important decision after the Chicago loss that would also have a profound positive impact on the team for the remainder of the season.

Like the previous season, there had been a deep divide on the team over the quarterback situation. Coach Landry shuffled between Craig Morton and Roger Staubach, and his decision to pick Roger stabilized our team. It wasn't an easy decision for Coach Landry either.

Craig really fit what he considered a model quarterback for the Dallas offense, a strong guy who could stretch the defense on long pass routes. On the other hand, Roger was one of the few quarterbacks in the league whose ability to escape the pocket was just something that Coach Landry wasn't used to.

They were two extremely talented quarterbacks, but they were as different on the field as they were off it. Craig was a lot like my old roommate Don Meredith in that he enjoyed the nightlife. But it never affected his play on Sundays.

Roger was the complete opposite, whose strong Christian convictions matched those of Coach Landry. Our team was split over who should be the quarterback as well. Most of the offensive guys preferred Craig because of his big arm, while a lot of the players on defense had learned early on how difficult it was to try to stop Staubach.

At the end of the day, he picked Roger and the history of the Cowboys for the next decade was written. For the next seven weeks, we went undefeated, with the biggest win coming in Washington when we shut out the Redskins 13-0 to take over the lead in the East.

That game was especially memorable for me, because it was one of the few times we frustrated Sonny Jurgensen all afternoon, holding him to 76 yards passing, I made one of my personal favorite plays of the year, intercepting him and running it back 23 yards to help set up a score.

If Coach Landry had been skeptical about Roger running through defenses and getting injured, his mind was probably eased that day. Our only touchdown came when Roger broke out of the pocket, eluded tacklers all over the field, and ran it in from 29 yards out.

We controlled our own destiny after the Washington win. There wouldn't be any need for any more team meetings. The players knew we had the rare opportunity to play our way to the top of the NFL.

For the sixth consecutive year, we won our division, setting up our opening playoff game against the Minnesota Vikings at Municipal Stadium in Bloomington. The game was on Christmas Day, 1971, and the weather wasn't bad at all, with the temperature right at freezing.

It was a 6-3 game at the half, but a pair of second-half touchdowns, one on a run by Duane Thomas and other on a pass from Staubach to Hayes, gave us a 20-3 lead. The Vikings tried to get back in it, scoring on a safety and a touchdown pass, but we prevailed 20-12, setting up the first-ever playoff game at Texas Stadium in Irving.

For the second straight season, our opponent for the right to go to the Super Bowl was the San Francisco 49ers, and again it turned into a defensive struggle. If the 1970 game had been a nightmare experience for John Brodie, he really had one in the rematch.

We sacked him four times and intercepted three of his passes. For the second straight year, I picked him off, running it back 23 yards to help set up one of our two touchdowns in a 14-3 victory. Safety Cliff Harris and defensive end George Andrie got the other two interceptions.

Our defensive front pressured him all day, and we held the high-powered 49er offense to just over 200 yards. In the five games leading up to the Super Bowl, our defense had allowed only two touchdowns, so our confidence level was certainly high.

There is no question that having played in Super Bowl V, and more importantly, having gone through the two weeks leading up to it, helped us prepare to win Super Bowl VI. It became a mission for the Dallas Cowboy organization to make sure we didn't repeat all the mistakes we had made in Miami.

The coaching staff sequestered us in the hotel, and we weren't bothered with the barrage of fans. Our phones were cut off at night, and the ticket manager handled all requests, so we didn't have to worry with that in New Orleans.

Like I mentioned earlier, I thought that Coach Landry had prepared us the year before to play a game on the Sunday before the Super Bowl, and we peaked way too early emotionally. It's hard for me to explain in layman's terms about peaking emotionally, but anyone who plays or played football understands how much of a mental game it is.

When we went out on the field in old Tulane Stadium to play the Miami Dolphins, we were mentally and physically ready to play at our highest level.

I always prided myself in preparing for opponents through studying everything I could about them. As soon as we had won the NFC and found out we were playing the Dolphins, I spent many a night rolling those old tapes, trying to pick up any tendencies of their offense to tip off what plays Miami might run.

Miami Coach Don Shula had built his team around the best running attack in football, featuring Larry Csonka, Mercury Morris and Jim Kiick. I felt if we forced their quarterback, Bob Griese, to throw and if we could effectively cover Paul Warfield, their All-Pro receiver, we could shut down their offense.

In watching the films, I had noticed some alignments that tipped off which back was going to get the ball. Our coaches also devised a brilliant strategy to take Warfield out of the game. Our two cornerbacks, Mel Renfro and Herb Adderley – both future Hall-of-Famers – could cover anybody.

Our game plan was for Renfro to cover Warfield wherever he went with an assisting hand from our great safety Cornell Green. I tell you Cornell was one of the best defensive backs ever in football. He had been a basketball starter at Utah State and had signed as a free agent by Gil Brandt in 1962.

He had been an All-Pro cornerback before moving to safety. In the Super Bowl, he not only had the assignment of doubling up on Warfield, but he was critical to our strategy of stopping their running attack. Mel and Cornell did a job of neutralizing Warfield.

As a sidebar, President Richard Nixon had called Don Shula earlier in the week and offered up a pass play to Warfield. The president assured Shula it would work, but when Miami ran Presidents Nixon's play in the third quarter, Renfro batted the ball harmlessly to the turf.

There was no doubt that Miami had an outstanding football team. The Dolphins would prove it by winning the next two Super Bowls, including having a perfect season in 1972. They hadn't backed into Super Bowl VI either, having defeated the defending champion Baltimore Colts before winning the longest game in NFL history, a 27-24 overtime game against the Kansas City Chiefs.

Regardless of Miami's success, I thought we were the better team, and we were determined to prove it on the field.

We never trailed in the game. We took a first-quarter lead on a field goal by Mike Clark, then scored on a 76-yard drive that featured Calvin Hill's running and two completions from Staubach to Alworth, including a seven-yard touchdown.

Miami did score a field goal on the last play of the half, but it was a big-time play by Green that kept the Dolphins from having a touchdown. Griese had Warfield wide open at the two-yard line, and it seemed like a sure TD. Somehow, Cornell knocked the ball away, forcing a Garo Yepremian field goal.

One of the most unforgettable plays in Super Bowl history came in the first half, and it was made by our defense. Griese went back to pass from the Miami 38, and three of our defensive linemen broke through and started chasing him.

Bob Lilly, Larry Cole and Jethro Pugh chased Griese inside the 10-yard line where Bob finally caught him for a 29-yard loss. It's still the record for the most yards lost on a single play in Super Bowl history.

Coach Landry made a tactical change in our offensive strategy at the half that broke the game wide open. We felt confident that if we scored one more touchdown, Miami was in deep trouble.

We had been able to run the ball inside the tackles with a lot of success in the first half, so Coach Landry decided we'd go outside during the second half. The first time we had the ball, we drove 71 yards, almost all on the ground. Duane Thomas got most of them, but a flanker reverse to Bob Hayes picked up 16 yards to keep the Dolphins reeling.

Thomas got the touchdown to make it 17-3 and Chuck Howley pretty much ended the game with an interception that he returned to the Miami nine. We kidded Chuck after the game, because he had a cinch touchdown but tripped on his way to the end zone. Mike Ditka was the benefactor, because he caught a touchdown pass from Roger that gave us a 24-3 lead. That's how it would end.

There were a lot of smiles and happy faces on the sideline and in the locker room. Even stoic Coach Tom Landry started beaming when he was carried off the field as the final seconds ticked off. Personally, I was happy, but I was also relieved that the Dallas Cowboys had finally won the world championship of football.

There was no doubt it was a game that we won the old-fashioned way with our offense running the ball and our defense shutting down the heralded Miami running attack. We rushed for a Super Bowl record 252 yards and held the Dolphins to 80 on the ground.

Csonka, who would have an MVP afternoon in the Super Bowl two years later, netted only 40 yards against us.

While we had excellent running backs and explosive players in our passing attack to go with one of the best defensive teams in the NFL, there were some guys who helped pave the way to our success without much credit: the Dallas offensive line.

During that era, we had one of the best offensive lines around. When we overpowered Miami with our running attack, those guys all should have been awarded game balls for the way they played as a unit. Ralph Neely and Rayfield Wright were our tackles, John Niland and Blaine Nye the guards, and our center was Dave Manders. Mike Ditka and Billy Truax were the two tight ends.

All of those players were seasoned veterans by the time we got to the Super Bowl, and their role of making Dallas a champion should never be minimized. I can tell you from experience during my early years as a Cowboy, I didn't think our guys on offense were very tough. But that all changed as these men were either drafted or traded for to join our team.

Our defense dominated the game in a fashion that few have in the history of the Super Bowl. It's still the only one in which a team didn't score a touchdown, and the Dolphins managed only 10 first downs in the game.

Cornell Green probably summed it up best. He said that we were there on a mission to win the Super Bowl, while the Dolphins were just happy to have played their way to New Orleans.

Our win wasn't without controversy. Duane Thomas, who had an outstanding game, rushing for a game high 95 yards and catching three passes, had refused to talk to the media during the press conferences during the week., Many experts thought his silence cost him the MVP.

In the post-game interview, one of the analysts, Tommy Brookshier – who had been a standout defensive back for the Eagles – asked Duane, "You have great speed, don't you, Duane?"

Thomas had a one-word answer: "Evidently."

Despite his immense talents on the field, I think everyone figured that his days as a Cowboy were limited. In 1970 Gil Brandt and the Cowboys had made a bold first round-draft pick when they selected the running back from West Texas State. He was a gifted athlete, with the skills to be a game breaker on offense to match our ability to strike from anywhere on the field with our passing game.

Duane not only brought athleticism to our offense, he also brought an attitude that was frankly difficult for most of us to accept, including Coach Landry. In retrospect, there is no doubt that Coach and Duane had a strained relationship, and that's probably being the nicest way I can describe it.

On the field, Duane was the offensive catalyst who helped get us into two Super Bowls and win the second one. If he had been around after the 1971 season, I think the history of Dallas Cowboy football would be remembered for more than just one championship during my final years as an NFL player.

Duane called Coach Landry the "plastic man." He referred to Tex Schramm as "demented, sick and dishonest." The front office and staff had enough of Duane and shipped him off to San Diego before the 1972 season. He played a couple of years for the Redskins before trying to come back and be a Cowboy a few years later, but he didn't make the team.

I believe that it's best to resolve problems you have with other people.

That's something I don't fear a bit. I called Duane a few years after he left the Cowboys and told him up front that I didn't appreciate the things he'd said when he left Dallas, but I wanted to have lunch with him and talk man to man.

And we did. I respected Duane as a player and I respected what he had to say. I came away with a respect for him that you only get when you lay it on the line. My only regret was that I hadn't taken the lead back in 1971 and tried to understand him better.

Before Coach Landry left Dallas in the late 1980s, Duane came back to training camp and they reconciled as well. Duane said something to the effect that he had learned what Coach Landry was trying to get across and without his leadership, he'd never have had the opportunity to play on a winning Super Bowl team for the Cowboys.

I am sure there are many professions where you gain insight into human nature, but I know you do in the game of football. Like I say, if Duane had been a Cowboy during those last years I was playing, I think we would have won some more championships. That's how good he was. Unfortunately, we just never quite had the running game again. Essentially, our running attack would become Roger Staubach scrambling.

TIME OUT: BOB LILLY

All-time great Bob Lilly talks about Lee Roy Jordan as a leader.

Lee Roy's credentials as a player speak for themselves. He missed a few games his first two years, then started for 12 straight seasons and played every game. A lot of times he was banged up enough that it would have kept a lot of players on the sidelines. Not Lee Roy. Lee Roy went to a bunch of Pro Bowls and made All-NFL teams, but it was his leadership ability that set him apart from other players.

How good a leader was he? All I can say is if I were to go to war, I'd want him to be my captain. He's the best leader a defensive team could ever have.

He was the one player who kept the team together after all those tough losses in the championship games. Lee Roy was the one player who was going to play at his best, whether it was in the Ice Bowl or whether as a team we were just playing lousy in playoff losses to Cleveland.

Those were hard to battle back from, but the loss in Super Bowl V was especially tough. We just gave the game away. I think there was a lot of self-doubt after that among our players. Were we ever going to win the championship?

When we returned for training camp in the summer of 1971, Lee Roy got us together and told us, "We are going to give 110 percent in every practice and every game until we win the Super Bowl."

He would actually chew us out. He'd yell at me, "Bob, you aren't running to the ball." And, I made sure I did on the next play.

After we gave away a couple of games in the regular season, it was Lee Roy who rallied us. We went on to win the NFC championship and earned the right to play the Miami Dolphins in Tulane Stadium in New Orleans.

We knew the ropes at the Super Bowl, and everyone was determined not to repeat the mistakes that we had made the year before.

Mr. Murchison had security all over the hotel, so nothing would interrupt our routine. There were no distractions this time. Miami probably was in the same boat we were in the year before, and trust me, it was – and still is – a learning experience.

Miami had a great team, with a rushing attack that averaged more than 200 yards a game, and their No-Name Defense was just as good.

We all watched a lot of film on Miami for the two weeks leading up to the game, but no one did more than Lee Roy. He noticed splits between the center and guards that would tip off where the ball was going. During the game, he would call out our names to let us know if the play was coming our way.

Miami could do nothing running the ball, and a lot had to do with Lee Roy being so prepared. He had a sixth sense about him on the football field. He had the ability to just know what they were going to do. Just like he did for 12 years, Lee Roy called all the defensive signals. I don't know if he ever had a better day than he did in New Orleans.

Winning that game was like taking a 1000-pound weight off our backs. We were all tired of the nicknames like "Bridesmaids of the NFL" and "Next Year's Champion." Winning the Super Bowl meant we would always be champions.

We certainly didn't make the kind of money then that players make today. But I think we had something that money couldn't buy and that was a strong bond as a team, because we stayed together on and off the field.

Heck, we even car-pooled to practice, because most of us only had one car and our wives would use it to drive the kids around. After a game, we'd go where a local beer distributor had a party room. It would just be the players and our families.

There was a juke box in the room to listen to music. The owner would feed us all the barbecue we could eat and have all kind of cold drinks for us. It was a great bonding time for not only the players but our families, and another reason we were so close.

Another Dallas Cowboy fan owned a Shakey's Pizza. He'd host us for free pizzas, beer and cold drinks. This was our entertainment after the game and how we celebrated winning games and commiserated with one another when we lost.

On our off days, I'd go quail, dove and duck hunting with Lee Roy and Walt Garrison. We'd go fishing together. We developed friendships on and off the field that lasted well past our playing days.

When we played our games at the Cotton Bowl, we'd stay outside the locker room and sign autographs. My dad would bring us something to drink, and we'd stay there until the last fan left. I think that's how we helped built a special connection with the Cowboy fans. You rarely see that today.

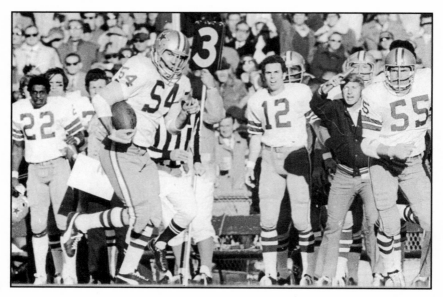

Chuck Howley (54) heads down the field after intercepting a pass. Roger Staubach (12) looks on while I look for someone to block.

Coach Landry giving instructions in practice.

CHAPTER 18
TRANSITION OF THE COWBOYS BEGINS

Although I think most people expected the Cowboys to continue to control the NFC East and go to the Super Bowl just about every year, no team – regardless of its talent – is not invincible. Obviously, ours started with Duane Thomas and his inability to fit into what Coach Landry and the Cowboys expected. After he held out in the summer, he was traded to the New England Patriots.

Since we still had Calvin Hill, who was healthy after returning from back and knee injuries, our running attack was still an asset. We still had Walt Garrison at fullback as well as a rookie from Houston, Robert Newhouse.

Another addition to the Cowboys was Gene Stallings. Coach Stallings had been one of the Alabama coaches who had scouted me back at Excel High School. After the 1964 season, he became head coach at Texas A&M and led the Aggies to the 1967 Southwest Conference championship.

He had been fired after the 1971 season in College Station and landed a job as the secondary coach in Dallas thanks to an assist from Coach Bryant, who assured Coach Landry he was getting a top-level coach.

On the field, injuries and a team that was getting older started showing in the results. During the pre-season schedule in a game against the Rams, Roger Staubach went down with a shoulder injury and was lost for most of the season.

Not only was Roger one of the best quarterbacks, if not the best, in the NFL, his leadership skills were immeasurable. You couldn't find a finer person anywhere. Roger and I had become roommates, and I think the two of us shared that common trait of preparing totally for a game. We prided ourselves in being the captains of the offense and the defense, and we prided ourselves in being completely aware of everything an opponent might throw at us on Sunday.

Craig Morton was still on the team and certainly had the experience to step right back into that starting role. He'd led us to one Super Bowl, and his arm strength and ability to move us down the field were indeed reminiscent of Don Meredith.

Despite their immense skills, our two receivers – Bob Hayes and Lance Alworth – were both on the back halves of their Hall of Fame careers and didn't strike the fear into secondaries like they had during their earlier seasons.

During the 1972 season, they combined for a total of 30 catches for less than 400 yards, and Lance caught the only two touchdown passes between them. Since Calvin Hill led the team with 43 catches, I think that pretty much illustrates the problems we had getting the ball down the field, a Cowboy trademark for more than a decade.

Defensively, we suffered a blow when Bob Lilly played injured the entire season, and even though he made All-Pro, it was obvious that he was struggling just to make it through the games. It was bad enough that he injured his back, but Bob was also playing with a bone spur on his ankle and a bad knee. I don't even know how he got on the field, but that's the type of competitor he was.

Another problem we had was the emergence of the Washington Redskins as our chief rival for the best team in the East, a division we had virtually owned since our rise to power in 1966. George Allen, who had been the head coach of the Rams and the man who had gotten into the dispute with Tex Schramm about the spying incident back then, was now the Washington coach.

While our rivalry with Washington had always been intense, it escalated to a higher and more bitter level during those days. There was no love lost between the two franchises and there would be some real slugfests between the two teams during that era when Allen was the Redskin coach.

In 1972 we would play Washington three times, twice in the regular season and again in the playoffs. After the 1972 game in Dallas on December 9, I guess I made the big time, at least as far as media attention was concerned.

I appeared on the cover of *Sports Illustrated*. We won the Washington game at Texas Stadium, 34-24, in a game that Garrison and Hill both rushed for more than 100 yards. Actually, we led 31-10 in the fourth quarter before the Redskins rallied behind their quarterback Billy Kilmer.

That had been a troubling trend throughout the season, our inability to finish teams off. Regardless, the Cowboys were riding high again. We were one game behind the Redskins in the standings and no one was talking about the *Sports Illustrated* jinx. Supposedly, if you appeared on the cover, then something bad was going to happen to you soon.

Maybe we should have been worried about it. Despite Washington losing on the final weekend, we were no better, losing at home to the New York Giants. The Redskins had won the East, ending our six-year streak of winning the division.

We did qualify for the playoffs, having earned a spot as the wildcard team, forcing us to travel to San Francisco to play the 49ers. Much like the Cowboys, the 49ers had suffered their only injury problems that year, with John Brodie missing most of the season, and being replaced by Steve Spurrier.

When we got to the San Francisco game, Brodie was back on the field and no doubt ready to avenge the 49er playoff losses to the Cowboys the previous two seasons. Somebody wrote it was one of Dallas' greatest wins. I don't know about that.

We did come back, thanks in large part to Roger Staubach, who came off the bench when we trailed 28-13 in the fourth quarter and rallied us to a 30-28 victory. His touchdown passes to Billy Parks and Ron Sellers forever sealed Roger's legacy as one of the great comeback quarterbacks in NFL history.

Our safety Charlie Waters picked off two of Brodie's passes, and once again we had shut down the aerial attack of the 49ers.

Our improbable fourth-quarter rally coupled with the Redskins' 16-3 win over the Green Bay Packers set up the third match-up of the season with the Cowboys and our friends in the East. Unfortunately for us, that meant traveling to RFK Stadium in Washington for the right to go back to the Super Bowl.

The game was played on New Year's Eve, and it was only a game for a half. Washington led 10-3 at the break and went on to win 26-3. Roger quarterbacked the whole game, but we just couldn't move it in the air. Kilmer was effective enough against our defense to get the Redskins two touchdowns and four field goals.

Two weeks later, Miami – the team we had beaten in the Super Bowl a year earlier – made history when the Dolphins beat the Redskins, 14-7, becoming the only team in NFL history to post a perfect season.

As far as Dallas, there was no question that the Cowboys were a team in transition with that playoff loss in Washington exposing some of our problems. We still had a lot of gifted players, but I think the reality that a lot of us were on the back halves of our careers began to hit home.

After the season, Lance Alworth retired, making it important to find a quality receiver. Gil Brandt pulled one of the great coups of his career when he signed a free agent from Tulsa, Drew Pearson, who would eventually be the go-to receiver for Roger Staubach.

Drew had started out as a quarterback in college before being converted to a receiving spot. Even though he starred at Tulsa, he went undrafted.

Gil signed him to a Cowboy contract, and he was so good that he would be named as one of the receivers on the NFL All-Decade team for the 1970s. He would also become a team captain just to show what type of leadership skills he brought to our summer camp.

Alworth wasn't the only Cowboy to retire. Tight ends Mike Ditka and Billy Truax did as well, so a rookie out of Michigan State named Billy Joe Dupree was drafted in the first round to replace them.

Overall, the team had much the same look. With a healthy Staubach and Bob Lilly, our expectations were high that we would battle our way back into the Super Bowl.

On November 4, I had a game that I guess is a linebacker's dream when we beat the Cincinnati Bengals at Texas Stadium. Ken Anderson was the Bengal quarterback and was generally recognized as one of the better signal callers in the league.

He had a fast receiver, Isaac Curtis, who spread the field for them, but Ken also liked to throw to his backs, especially Bobbie Clark and Essex Johnson. We had them scouted well, and in the first quarter of the game, I intercepted Anderson three times, which I think was an NFL record.

I returned one of them 31 yards for a touchdown. The other two set up scores with a field goal by Toni Fritsch and a touchdown pass from Roger to Bob Hayes. We would go on to win the game 38-10, setting up yet again some decisive weekends to win the East.

In one of the most anticipated games of the year, we hosted the Miami Dolphins on Thanksgiving Day. I'm sure Pete Rozelle and his scheduling staff wanted to match up the last two Super Bowl champions, knowing it would be a TV bonanza for the league.

The game was expected to be a defensive struggle, despite featuring Hall of Fame quarterbacks Roger Staubach and Bob Griese. It lived up to its billing, although Miami jumped ahead 14-0 in the first quarter, thanks to a short run by Larry Csonka and a long pass to Paul Warfield.

After that, Miami didn't do much on offense the rest of the day, but the lead held up. We scored on a run by Walt Garrison in the fourth quarter, but we never could get close enough to threaten again. The final was 14-7, leaving us a game behind the Redskins with three to play.

We showed our championship mettle by winning our final three games and qualifying for the playoffs for the eighth straight season. Our 27-16 win over the Redskins pushed us to the top of the NFC East.

Dallas was back in the NFC Championship Game and our opponent was the Minnesota Vikings. Even though the game was played in Dallas, the Vikings dominated us, winning 27-10 to earn a spot against Miami in the Super Bowl.

At the end of season, I was chosen as the NFL's Defensive Player of the Year by the 101 Club and went to my fifth Pro Bowl. Despite those recognitions, the loss to the Vikings in the championship game hurt.

It was also the end of the line for my old teammate and close friend Chuck Howley. When I joined the Cowboys, Chuck was the strongside linebacker. He later moved over to the weak side where he just had an incredible career, being a Super Bowl MVP and a turnover machine for the defense.

Chuck had torn up his left knee during the regular season game at Washington in 1972 when he got clipped on a crack-back block. He tried a comeback in '73, but he knew he couldn't do the job any longer.

Another former SEC linebacker, D.D. Lewis, took over, giving the Cowboys a rarity of having three guys from the same conference starting at linebacker. While I was in the middle, I had an Auburn friend Dave Edwards on my strong side and Mississippi State grad D.D. on the weak.

There would be more transitions to come during the 1974 season and I knew that there weren't many more games left in a lot of us.

I did decide that it was time for me to man up to Tex Schramm and ask for a contract that would be financially beneficial to me and my family. I had talked to some other players from around the league, and I knew the Cowboys weren't paying any of us our market value.

I wanted a contract for $75,000 a year for three years. Tex Schramm absolutely went berserk and told me, "We aren't even paying Roger Staubach that much." I said something back like, "Well, you should be."

And, they should have been. I felt the same about all those other great players who had helped build the Cowboys into a dynasty and one of the NFL's most valuable properties.

I did what I thought was right, and still do. I have no regrets whatsoever. I got my raise, too.

TIME OUT: CORNELL GREEN

Cornell Green was a two-time All-American basketball player at Utah State. Drafted to play in the NBA, Green opted to sign a contract with the Dallas Cowboys in 1962. He would become one of the greatest defensive backs in NFL history during his 13-year career, playing both cornerback and safety.

I signed to play for Dallas in 1962, thanks to Gil Brandt, who had scouted me playing basketball at Utah State. He thought I had the athletic ability to play in the NFL. To say I'm thankful would be an understatement.

Playing for the Cowboys in those early years and watching the team develop into what has become "America's Team" was special. Certainly, we had no idea the brand would become so popular.

As players, we knew we were building something special on the field, especially defensively. After my rookie year, Lee Roy Jordan came in as a first-round pick in 1963, and immediately he made an impact on the team. He was the consummate teammate, on and off the field.

We all had a goal of becoming the best team in the NFL, and Lee Roy was the type of player who pushed everyone hard to make sure that happened. We had a lot of outstanding young defensive players in the early 1960s, so I think we could all see us developing into the gold standard in the NFL.

By 1966, we were maturing into a team that had the ability to win it all, but I'm not sure if we really believed we had totally arrived. When we won the Eastern Conference that year, Dallas was on the cusp of being the best, and we stayed there for the rest of my career.

Lee Roy was the defensive captain of those teams, and the reason was pretty simple. He was the quarterback, the man who called the signals. He was the man who played with intensity every practice and every game.

The two losses to the Packers to end our 1966 and 1967 seasons were tough on all of us, particularly Lee Roy. But you know what, he showed class in defeat. That's not easy to do, especially the way we lost those two games.

It was particularly frustrating because we missed on the chance to play in the first two Super Bowls.

I learned a lot from him on the way he handled himself in defeat. I think his ability to bounce back from the losses served as a catalyst for us until we did reach the Super Bowl.

We should have won Super Bowl V, so finally being crowned champions after we beat Miami in Super Bowl VI was a defining moment for all of us. I know in the win over the Dolphins, I had one of my best games, because I had double duty of helping stop Paul Warfield and stopping the run.

Lee Roy probably did his best job ever of getting the defense ready, because the Dolphin run attack was the best in the NFL. We shut them down. We weren't going to lose that game. I think it was a collective attitude of our team because we had a special bond like you rarely see.

When you played for the Cowboys, you represented your family, your teammates, your organization. No team did so any better than that 1971 group. We believed in each other and believed in our goal.

After I retired after the 1974 season, I stayed involved in football as a scout, and I remained friends with my teammates. Lee Roy and I have been friends since we lined up together during those hot summer practices in 1963. You never forget a man like that, because he symbolizes everything that is good about football and being a man.

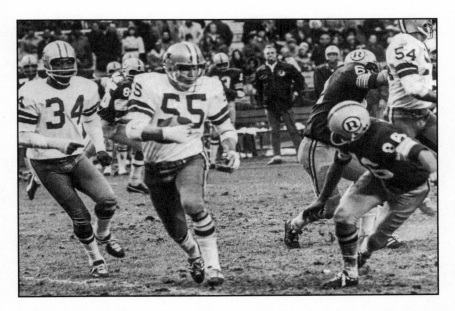

Having played with Cornell Green (34) and Chuck Howley (54) for so many years made me appreciate greatness.

TIME OUT: RAYFIELD WRIGHT

Rayfield Wright was drafted by the Dallas Cowboys in 1967 as a tight end prospect. By his own admission, basketball was his primary sport. At Fort Valley State, Wright played both, becoming a basketball legend with his 28-point, 20-rebound average. The old Cincinnati Royals of the NBA drafted him to play alongside Oscar Robertson. He never made it to camp, instead going to Dallas and becoming a football legend and a good friend with Lee Roy Jordan.

Gil Brandt drafted me as a tight end and I joined 137 rookies trying to make the Cowboy roster in the summer of 1967. My mother and grandmother didn't want me to play football and never saw a game I played. They wanted me to play basketball.

I told them I'd go see if I could make the Cowboys and if I didn't, I'd go to camp at Cincinnati. The rest I guess you could say is history. Only five of those rookies made the team. I think one of the reasons I did is I was serious and I wanted to emulate players who were serious about football.

Two guys who stood out to me were Lee Roy Jordan and Bob Lilly. Even though both of them were defensive players, I knew they were leaders and they embraced the young Cowboys and did whatever they could to make us better players.

Lee Roy taught me so much about being a professional athlete and the Cowboy way. I really think the number one thing was that the team always mattered more than the individual. He was about winning and being totally prepared.

When Coach Tom Landry told me that he thought I could be an All-Pro at tackle, I trusted him. I'd played tight end the first few years and had never played tackle in my life.

Lee Roy was the one player who encouraged me more than anyone. He would come up to me and say, "Rayfield, I know you can do it."

He made the teammates believe. Lee Roy was a captain for a reason and I admired him so much as a player, leader and person. He took me under his wing and helped me become a captain with him.

Coach Landry expected the captains to handle the player problems unless they became so intense and magnified that the coaches and the management had to handle them. Lee Roy never backed down in his charge to be a leader.

When there was a problem among players, he'd solve it. That's just a fact. As a player Lee Roy had few peers, then or now. He was an exceptional athlete, who had great quickness, but even more importantly an intuition to get us in the right defense. This guy just never seemed to have a breakdown.

The Dallas way was to have great athletes with quickness and football smarts. For example, our offensive linemen pulled all the time. Coach Landry told me that I'd be great pulling not necessarily because I had good speed but because I had quickness. Quickness was a necessity for all the Cowboy players, and Lee Roy had plenty of that, too.

Lee Roy could have easily been a star at outside linebacker or safety, but if there was ever a man born to play middle linebacker – particularly in the Dallas Flex Defense – it was him.

Although he wasn't the biggest middle linebacker, he was the toughest and quickest and smartest one around. He never missed a practice or a game his last 12 seasons. Think about that. You'd know he was hurting but he'd be on the field every day, giving every ounce of effort he had.

A football team is like a car. You can have the best-looking car with all the best parts from the wheels to all the electronic gadgets to whatever. But you have to have an engine to make that car run, and Lee Roy Jordan was the motor of the Doomsday Defense.

In 1972, I was voted the best offensive lineman in the NFL. Lee Roy told me that meant I had to practice even harder and give even more effort. The reason was simple. When you are regarded as being the best in the NFL, the guy opposite you on Sunday is going to play with even more intensity and try to knock you off that pedestal.

Lee Roy faced the same challenge. He was regarded as being an elite middle linebacker and he was making more tackles than anyone in football. The offensive linemen would try to whip him every Sunday, but most of the time they got it handed to them by this man.

When I think back on those days when everyone said we couldn't win the big games, it was Lee Roy that was the glue that held us together. Sure, we thought about all the bad breaks that seemed to go our way in those games. Lee Roy kept telling us that when we get knocked down, get back up and go back after them.

When we lost to Baltimore in the Super Bowl, man, that was tough. We had the game basically won when we fumbled on the goal line and our center Dave Manders came out of the pile with the ball and handed it to the official. The films of the game were conclusive that Dave had recovered Duane Thomas' fumble and we should have retained the ball. The officials ruled otherwise and gave it to Baltimore.

People ask me about that play, and I tell them I was too busy trying to block Bubba Smith to have seen Dave recover it, but he did.

We had a tough time getting mentally over that particular game, but because of Lee Roy's leadership and determination, we did just that and won it the next year.

I feel awfully blessed to have played with the Cowboys and to have had a teammate and friend like Lee Roy Jordan. That man helped instill confidence in me when I was a young guy trying to find my way in the NFL.

CHAPTER 19
END OF AN ERA; THE BEGINNING OF ANOTHER

I f there were ever seasons of changes for the Dallas Cowboys, 1974 and 1975 were two that would ring out the end of one era and the beginning of a new one. I wish I could say 1974 was a season to remember mainly because of our successes on the field. But it would be memorable because of saying goodbye to old friends, players that I'd played with for a decade and one who had brought so much triumph and joy to the Dallas fans.

Bob Lilly, the anchor of our defense and eventually voted to the all-time NFL team, decided to retire after the season as did fullback Walt Garrison and center Dave Manders. Dan Reeves, who had been a backup the previous few years, had moved into a full-time coaching role by 1974, and Bob Hayes would move on to San Francisco after '74 to try to rejuvenate his career as a 49er.

Calvin Hill played his final year in Dallas that season before signing to play with the Hawaiian team in the new World Football League. Guard John

Niland and defensive end Pat Toomay were traded after the season to the Eagles and Bills.

Craig Morton, who had given it his all as the man who replaced Don Meredith and then lost his job to Roger Staubach, was traded to the Giants. There were some new faces in 1974, most noticeably this gigantic defensive end from Tennessee State, Ed "Too Tall" Jones, and quarterback Danny White, the heir apparent to Roger.

The season started off about as bad as it could get. After we beat Atlanta on opening Sunday 24-0, we proceeded to lose four straight games. All four were decided by a touchdown or less, but coming close doesn't win championships. For the first time since the early 1960s, Dallas was 1-4 and seemingly out of the race for playoff contention.

When we lost by a touchdown to Washington in mid-November, we were 5-5 and about our only hope of making the playoffs was to win the rest of our games. We trailed both the Redskins and St. Louis Cardinals by two games entering the final four weekends of the season.

After we shut out Houston in the Astrodome 10-0, we had a chance to make up a game against the Redskins at Texas Stadium on Thanksgiving Day. It would become a memorable game, more so for a one-hit wonder quarterback Clint Longley than anything else.

Longley had gone to college at Abilene Christian as a walk-on. His strong arm caught the attention of some NFL scouts and he was drafted by the Bengals before being traded to the Cowboys. With Craig Morton shipped off to the Giants, Clint became our back-up quarterback and he quickly earned the nickname "The Mad Bomber."

His passes could go a long way, but you never knew where they would land. One day in practice, he hit Coach Landry's coaching tower and that's how he got the nickname.

By the time we played the Redskins, he'd never set foot on the field for a game. He wouldn't have that day either if Roger had been healthy. He had entered the game battling the flu and then had to leave in the third quarter after getting blindsided on an attempted pass play.

When Roger left the game, I don't think anyone had much hope of us of winning. We were down 16-3 late in the third quarter and the Washington defense was having its way with our offense. Defensively, we had done a good job of keeping them to field goals until Billy Kilmer completed a touchdown pass to our old running back Duane Thomas.

Then, magic happened in the form of Longley and an improbable fourth quarter rally that forever sealed his legacy as a one-time Thanksgiving wonder. Longley marched us to two touchdowns, one on a pass to Billy Joe Dupree and the second setting up a short run by Walt Garrison to give us a 17-16 lead.

If we thought we had the game won, well the Redskins had different ideas. Kilmer drove Washington down the field and Thomas finished off the drive with a touchdown run and the Redskins were back on top 23-17.

Our defense made several big plays. After we lost a fumble deep in our own territory, the Redskins needed only a field goal to put it away, but Ed Jones used his height to block their attempt and keep us alive.

After Drew Pearson fumbled a pass from Longley, it looked even bleaker. There wasn't much time left but we stopped them and forced a punt with under two minutes to go in the game. With 30 seconds left and no timeouts, Longley launched a pass to Pearson on a post pattern and he was wide open 50 yards down the field for the winning touchdown.

Naturally, the media made a big deal about Longley and his future greatness. It never happened. He only threw a few more passes as a Cowboy, getting a start against the Jets on the last weekend of the 1975 season when Roger was banged up. He was long gone before the start of my final year in 1976.

Roger was the consummate team player and a super athlete. Roger could bounce the football off the ground and it would come right back to him. That's not easy to do, and Clint tried to do it and just couldn't get the ball to bounce back to him. He just couldn't seem to be better than Roger in anything, and tensions seemed to grow.

After a practice in the summer of 1976, Longley was making some derogatory remarks about Drew Pearson in the locker room because Drew had dropped one of his passes during the drills. Roger didn't like it, and told him so. Well, they agreed to have it out on the baseball field near the practice field.

By the time Dan Reeves got there to break them up, Roger had Clint on the ground, whipping up on him. Let me say this, while there is a great bond among players, there will naturally be conflicts as well. And no doubt, there was a rift on the offensive side of the ball.

I wish that was the end of the story. But later on in the locker room, Longley sucker-punched Roger, knocking him into some scales and cutting him in the process. It didn't happen far from me and some of us quickly moved over to stop the fight from getting worse.

All I could think was, "What the heck is this guy doing?"

It didn't take long for the Cowboy organization to react. Coach Landry had had enough. Gil Brandt got on the phone immediately, working on a trade with San Diego. I think Longley's bags were packed by the time he got ready to leave the facility. He was indeed on his way to San Diego.

That sucker punch may have been one of the most fortuitous moves in the history of pro football. Gil Brandt pulled off a lot of great trades and draft choices in his career, but he topped them all with this one.

Dallas got a draft pick for Longley that would help land Tony Dorsett – the Heisman-winning tailback from Pittsburgh – in the 1977 draft. As they say, the rest is history.

It's hard not to talk about the 1974 season without mentioning the Washington Thanksgiving game, because it has become part of football lore. Our win over them was one of the bright spots of the season, because we lost on the final weekend to Oakland to miss out on the playoffs for the first time in nine years.

The Raiders beat us 27-23, thanks mainly to the play of their quarterback

Kenny "Snake" Stabler. Kenny was a gifted quarterback with that unique ability to make plays in the clutch and he made several that day. He threw three touchdown passes, but I did have my moment against Kenny when I intercepted a pass that helped set up one of our scores.

It would be the only time I ever played against Kenny, but we became good friends over the years. When I'd see him, I would joke with him about being one of his favorite receivers that day in Oakland. He would grin and say something to the effect that he wanted an old Alabama boy to look good.

When the 1974 season ended, the mass exodus of some of the most legendary names in Cowboy history began. It set in motion one of the most unforgettable drafts in football history, and perhaps the shining moment in Gil Brandt's own legendary career as a team builder.

Dallas' draft became known as "The Dirty Dozen" because 12 picks made the team that season and didn't even include linebacker Mike Hegman, who was drafted in the seventh round as a future pick. He couldn't report until 1976 and he ended up playing 12 years with the Cowboys.

Another player who was signed as a free agent was quarterback Jim Zorn, who ended up becoming a record-setting passer for the Seattle Seahawks.

In the first round, Dallas had two picks and chose a defensive tackle from Maryland, Randy White, and an outside linebacker from Langston University, Thomas "Hollywood" Henderson. The third-round pick from Arizona State, Bob Breunig, would eventually become the man who replaced me at middle linebacker.

I knew that I was in the twilight of my career, and I felt a responsibility to be a mentor to the young linebackers just like Jerry Tubbs had been to me back in 1963. Randy White was one of the most gifted football players I'd ever seen, and because of his size and speed, the coaches thought he'd have the opportunity to succeed me.

If he couldn't, they'd move him back to the defensive line where he'd starred for the man who had first scouted me for Alabama, Jerry Claiborne. Bob was a natural inside linebacker, so I had a dual role as the Cowboys prepared for the 1975 season, first to help the team return to the playoffs and second to prepare one of these two young players to become my heir apparent.

In most regards, the 1975 season would be one of the most special ones of my career and for the Cowboys as well.

Lee Roy Jordan has done so much for me in my life that I really don't have enough good words to say about him. He is one of those men who was one of the greatest football players I ever had the honor of seeing, but he's truly a much better man, a real humanitarian.

When I signed as a free agent to play for Dallas, Lee Roy had already been the leader of the defense for a number of seasons. Maybe it's because we had similar backgrounds that we became instant friends.

I know he was the one Dallas Cowboy who welcomed me to the team. He kind of adopted me on and off the field, making sure I felt part of the organization.

One other thing we had in common was we were intense players, and I saw early on in practice how much it meant to him. You can say I took my cue on how to practice from Lee Roy.

On the field, I think defensive players have short memories and don't remember every play like offensive players seem to recall. At least it was that way when I played. You just moved on to the next play and gave it everything you had.

There are a couple of moments I'll never forget about Lee Roy. One was in one of my first practices. We had this great young running back from Yale named Calvin Hill. He was 6-foot-4 and weighed 235 and could long jump 26 feet. He was some kind of athlete, big and strong and fast.

We were in a scrimmage and Calvin kind of tiptoed through the line and the next thing I know Lee Roy had just waylaid him with one of the hardest tackles I'd ever seen. I'm thinking, "Wow. This guy means business." I took my cue from how he practiced and played.

I like to think my intensity was one of my main assets, and in practice, I didn't mind popping one of our receivers when he went to catch the ball. I do think we made the offense tougher and better in Dallas. That was because of the way Lee Roy practiced, and we emulated him.

One other vivid memory I have on the field was against Cincinnati in 1973 when Lee Roy set the NFL record for most interceptions by a linebacker in a game. He had three in one quarter but one of those should have been mine! I was getting ready to intercept the Ken Anderson pass and the next thing I know, I see No. 55 flash in front of me and intercept my pass! If I ever got mad at Lee Roy, it was on that play.

I'm humbled to think back on my career and just think of all those great players I played with, including my fellow secondary teammates Cornell Green, Mel Renfro and Charlie Waters.

I think Coach Landry saw Lee Roy as an extension of himself. The system we had was the Flex Defense. It was a thinking man's defense and it was a perfect fit for Lee Roy. To play the Flex, you had to combine both mental and physical toughness, and Lee Roy had tons of that.

Lee Roy was a perfect leader for Coach Landry, not only because he had no reluctance to stand up and speak to Coach Landry, but he could voice the feelings of the rest of the team to him.

Coach Landry was an absolutely brilliant man, perhaps the best coach ever on football strategy on both offense and defense, but it was Lee Roy who always had a pulse beat of the entire team that Coach Landry just didn't have. Like I said, Coach Landry looked to Lee Roy to communicate the feelings of the team back to him.

Lee Roy was the captain for a reason. He was the catalyst for the years of dominance in the NFL, because in the very beginning, he took it upon himself to lead the team and make the Cowboys a champion.

I'll never forget being a rookie and standing in the huddle in the Cotton Bowl for my first game. I'm the only rookie starting, and I'm there with all these great players. Bob Lilly looked at me and said, "We are going to the Super Bowl, and don't screw it up, rookie." Lee Roy just nodded to make sure I got the message.

And, I remember being in RFK Stadium, a really hostile environment in one of those tough, tight games. Washington had the ball in a crucial situation and Lee Roy yelled out, "All right, we're going to stop them." It keyed everybody up, and we sure as hell stopped them.

I think it was his mental toughness that permeated throughout the team and we as a group fed off his words and actions. I know I feel unbelievably lucky to have lined up and played with Lee Roy Jordan.

CHAPTER 20
THE MEMORABLE 1975 SUPER BOWL TEAM

Maybe the 1975 season was a lucky 13 for me as a Dallas Cowboy. I was 34 years old, and I knew I didn't have many days left on the playing field. But I had one of my best years of my career, intercepting six passes and causing a couple of fumbles.

I also took my responsibilities to help develop Bob Breunig or Randy White as my eventual successor seriously. No one thought we were going to be very good that season, but we started off fast, winning our first four games and firmly placing us in the race for the Eastern Division championship.

We had opened with an 18-7 win against Los Angeles in a game in which Mel Renfro intercepted two passes and I got my first one of the year. Mel, like me, was near the end of his great career, but he still played like an All-Pro.

In an overtime win over the St. Louis Cardinals, I had another interception in that one, returning it 38 yards to set up a score. I think that win certainly built our hopes that we had a chance to be a good football team.

Late in the season, the Cardinals avenged that overtime loss, beating us 31-17 at Busch Stadium to win the East. That game illustrated our offensive problems for the 1975 and 1976 seasons, a lack of production from our running back position. Roger was our leading rusher in St. Louis, and obviously, those came on scramble plays.

Despite the loss, we had a chance to earn the wildcard spot if we could beat the Redskins in Dallas the next weekend. We had one of our best defensive performances of the season, winning 31-10.

I had my sixth interception of the season in that game, which was a team high. Charlie Waters picked off Billy Kilmer twice and returned one for a touchdown. Overall, our defense forced four turnovers and held Washington to just over 200 yards in offense.

Our final regular season game was at Shea Stadium in New York against the Jets and my old teammate Joe Namath. It was a sad day for me, watching Joe, thinking back to our days at Alabama and knowing that he was near the end of his career as well.

He only threw nine passes, before he left the game. We had already clinched a playoff spot, and Roger didn't play for us in a 31-21 win. Now, it was time to get ready for the playoffs.

Being back in the playoffs was a remarkable achievement, considering most of the experts didn't think we'd have a break-even season. Their reasoning was sound, because of the youth movement and overall inexperience of the team. Having to play the team with the best record in the entire NFL, the Minnesota Vikings at their stadium, didn't make our prospects of advancing look very good either.

The playoff win at old Metropolitan Stadium would be one of the most improbable in Dallas history and one of the most controversial, too. It was a cold afternoon and one that the Doomsday Defense of Dallas and the Purple People Eaters of Minnesota controlled.

The Vikings' longest play in the first half was a 16-yard scramble by Fran Tarkenton – the league's MVP in '75 – and Minnesota scored the only touchdown after a freak fumble was recovered near our goal line.

A Viking punt hit the ground near our return man Cliff Harris, just missing him. One of our blockers Pat Donovan thought it had touched Cliff and tried to recover it, but the football was recovered by Minnesota near the goal line. It was 7-0 at the half.

Eventually, the Cowboys would go ahead 10-7. We had two sustained drives, one resulting in a touchdown pass from Staubach to Dupree and the other a field goal by Toni Fritsch.

In the fourth quarter, Minnesota had its lone drive of the game. Tarkenton completed four passes to move them 70 yards and the Vikings went ahead 14-10.

All hopes of a comeback seemed over when they held us on the next drive, forcing us to punt. All Minnesota needed was a first down, but on third-and-two, Charlie Waters made one of the biggest plays of the year, breaking through and throwing Tarkenton for a loss.

Our offense had one last chance to go the length of the field and with no timeouts left. We'd seen Roger work magic before, but he really picked it up a notch on this final drive. On a fourth-and-16, Roger completed a 25-yard pass to Drew Pearson to give us a couple of more plays to pull off a miracle.

It would come on a 50-yard touchdown pass from Roger to Drew in the final seconds. That play was more than just a little bit controversial. The Vikings' Nate Wright had excellent coverage and claimed that Drew not only went out of bounds but pushed off as well.

Minnesota defensive end Alan Page was so mad that he slammed his helmet on the frozen ground, which drew a 15-yard penalty and forced the kickoff to be from midfield. What little hope the Vikings had ended on the penalty. We sacked Tarkenton on successive plays to end the game.

The whole scene was unreal. Whiskey bottles were flying from the stands, one hitting referee Armen Terzian in the head and knocking him out. I was just glad to get off the field with a victory and to the safety of the locker room.

In the post-game celebration, when asked about the winning touchdown, Roger said, "It was a Hail Mary pass." That term had never been used in football before but it became a part of football jargon. Every time I hear about the team heaving up a Hail Mary, I think back to that day in Minnesota.

We had to travel to Los Angeles to play the Rams for the NFL Championship and the right to play in Super Bowl X at the Orange Bowl in Miami.

That day belonged to our defense and Roger Staubach. We held the Rams to 122 yards, with only 18 coming on the ground, and Roger threw for four touchdowns in a 37-7 victory that made us the NFC champions.

D.D. Lewis was the star for the defense, intercepting two passes and setting up touchdowns for us after each one. While we had accomplished more than anyone thought we could, our ultimate challenge was trying to figure out a way to beat the powerful Pittsburgh Steelers.

Our 1975 team had one real weakness and that was our inability to run the football. Robert Newhouse was an effective fullback, but a lot of our running game came on scrambles by Roger. We certainly missed guys like Calvin Hill, but that is football, and we knew to beat the Steelers, we had to have another shutdown day by the Doomsday Defense.

That task wasn't going to be easy. Franco Harris and Rocky Bleier were a punishing one-two punch in the running game, and Pittsburgh quarterback Terry Bradshaw had two Hall of Fame receivers in John Stallworth and Lynn Swann.

Moving the football on the Steel Curtain Defense was going to be difficult with our running problems, but we had a lot of confidence that Roger would find a way to win us the game if we could hang tough.

We took the first lead of the game on our second drive when Roger hit Drew Pearson for a 29-yard touchdown. Pittsburgh quickly tied it 7-7 on a pass from Bradshaw to the tight end Randy Grossman.

We thought we had the drive stopped until Bradshaw hit Swann on a catch for a first down inside our 10. It would be the theme of the day, Swann making incredible catches that would ultimately be the difference in the game.

Other than Swann's amazing play, we really played well on defense throughout the afternoon. More than half the Steelers' yards came on long passes to Swann. Usually, we had excellent coverage on Swann from Mel Renfro and Cliff Harris. Lynn Swann was just that good that afternoon in Miami.

Going into the fourth quarter, we had a 10-7 lead and were playing about as well as we possibly could. Like all games, this one came down to a couple of plays, and unfortunately for the Cowboys, it was Swann who made them.

If Lynn was the thorn in our defense's side that day, their big defensive end L.C. Greenwood was a virtual nightmare for our offensive line, and Roger felt the brunt of it. The Steelers sacked him seven times, and I think Greenwood had five of them.

Game action shot in 1975.

Another real back-breaker for us came with less than 12 minutes left in the game when we were forced to punt from our own 16-yard line. Reggie Harrison blocked Mitch Hoopes' punt, resulting in a safety. It was 10-9 and Pittsburgh had all the momentum.

I want to say this about our defense. We really hung tough, being backed up on our next two drives and holding the Steelers to two field goals. It was also a case of the ball just bouncing the wrong way for us.

Bradshaw fumbled before the field goal that put the Steelers up 12-10, but it rolled out of bounds. On the next drive, Pittsburgh started on our seven after returning an interception inside the 10.

On third-and-goal from the one, I tackled Franco Harris, forcing a fumble, but again the Steelers recovered. It was a case of coming close. The big plays just as easily could have gone our way with any kind of luck.

Toss in the punt we had blocked in the fourth quarter and those plays were the difference in winning and losing. Pittsburgh won 21-17 but I know we laid it on the line and gave every bit of energy we had to win the game. Pittsburgh was just a little bit better than us and deserved to win the game.

It still hurt to lose, but I have nothing but fond memories of that season. Playing at the age of 34 is something that not many NFL linebackers manage to do, and I had enjoyed one of my best seasons. The only thing lacking was the Super Bowl ring.

TIME OUT: RANDY WHITE

After an All-American career with Maryland, Randy White was the first-round draft pick of Dallas in 1975. He would become a Hall of Fame defensive lineman and MVP in Dallas' Super Bowl win over Denver.

If there is one man that I looked up to during my NFL career, it was Lee Roy Jordan. I played down lineman at Maryland for Jerry Claiborne. I didn't find out until much later that he had been the same coach that discovered Lee Roy in high school and recommended him to Coach Bryant at Alabama.

Playing for Coach Claiborne helped prepare me to compete in the NFL, because he was not only a great coach and disciplinarian, but he demanded excellence on and off the field from his players. I guess it's fair to say that Lee Roy and I came from the same football family tree with Coach Claiborne being a protégé of his own mentor, Coach Bryant.

What I wasn't prepared for when I got to Dallas was playing middle linebacker.

When I was drafted in the first round, I was 6-foot-4, weighed 260 and ran a 4.6 40. I had been a fullback in high school and really wasn't highly recruited. At Maryland, I found my home on the defensive line.

In 1974, my senior year at Maryland, we'd played against Lee Roy's Crimson Tide and lost 21-16. Late in the game, I knocked the ball loose from Alabama quarterback Richard Todd and saw the ball rolling around but I couldn't get to it. I always thought if we had recovered Todd's fumble, we'd have won the game.

Certainly, playing well against Alabama helped my confidence in knowing I could play in the NFL, but I wasn't used to playing in a stand-up position at linebacker.

I was the second player picked in the 1975 draft, and I'm going to be a Cowboy. Well, I get to Dallas and the guy I've been brought into replace is Lee

Roy Jordan. You'd think he'd have been kind of standoffish for that reason, but he took me under his wing and became not only my friend but my mentor.

In 1975, there were 12 rookies that made the Cowboy roster, and the one person that every one of us looked up to and admired among the players and coaches was Lee Roy Jordan.

He worked endlessly with me, teaching me all the steps and nuances of being the middle linebacker in the Dallas Flex Defense. I would think to myself, "This guy is incredible." Eventually, I was moved back to defensive tackle, but the year I spent working with Lee Roy helped me have a better understanding of the total defensive concept of the Dallas Flex.

As a player, Lee Roy never made a mental mistake. He was always at the right spot at the right time. I was thinking, "If I'm ever half as good as he is, I'll be a heck of a player."

Lee Roy was always tutoring me about being a good football player and doing things the Cowboy way. There was an expectation that a Dallas Cowboy player excelled on and off the playing field. He'd say, "Randy, come on and ride with me."

We'd drive out to his ranch in Frisco, which is outside Dallas and where I now live. He would be teaching me all the way there and back.

When we'd get to his spread, he'd go out there and count his cows, and we'd talk about football and whatever else that was on our minds. My dad had been a butcher so I knew a little bit about cattle. But obviously Lee Roy had a passion for ranching when he was away from the football field.

There were a couple of moments my rookie year that I'll never forget. One of them was when we were in New York to play the Giants. Coach Landry had been a defensive back for the Giants back in the 1940s and 1950s, before becoming a renowned defensive coordinator for New York.

My locker was next to Bob Breunig, another rookie linebacker whom Lee Roy had adopted. Bob would eventually be the player to succeed him in the Cowboy defense. The concessionaires left game programs at our lockers.

Bob and I opened the program to the page where there was a picture of Coach Landry in his Giant uniform, and we were getting a laugh or two out of it.

We showed Lee Roy the picture of Coach Landry as a player, and I'll never forget him saying, "Well, look at old Terrible Tom with a head full of hair!"

Just as he said it, here comes Coach Landry walking up. Bob and I are climbing under our stools to avoid him. Lee Roy never missed a beat. He just looked up at Coach Landry and started talking defensive strategies for the game. Coach Landry didn't say a word to him either. Lee Roy is probably the only player that would have escaped Landry's wrath.

There was another time that year when Bob got called for roughing the punter. Mike Ditka was our special teams coach and had been a legendary tough guy as a tight end for the Bears and Cowboys.

Ditka was giving it to Breunig unmercifully. Well, Lee Roy had enough of it and went up to Ditka and told him to back off because Bob was giving it a 110 percent effort and had made a mistake.

Ditka didn't like it and the two of them squared off with each of them in the other's face. I really thought they were going to have a fight, and Coach Landry looked over at them. When those two saw Coach Landry staring at them, they just walked away. Such was the power of Coach Landry.

But, I think that's why Lee Roy was so popular with the players. When he didn't think you were giving it your all, he was quick to get on you. But when a player was giving it everything he had, Lee Roy was going to take up for you. I think that's why he was such a great leader and the players on the Cowboys admired him and would go to war for him.

Like I said, I never saw him make a mental mistake. But man, was he tough as well. He had unbelievable leverage, which enabled him to stand up the opposing guards on virtually every play and throw them backwards. Then he'd make the tackle.

Every chance I get I tell people one of the greatest travesties and mysteries to me is why this man is not in the Hall of Fame.

Lee Roy Jordan deserves to be in there and I can't understand why he isn't. I will never say a bad word about any player much less those who have gotten in the Hall of Fame, but in the years I played I didn't see a linebacker any better than Lee Roy, and quite a few of them are in the Hall.

With that being said, as great as he was as a football player, he's even a better man. I'm lucky to be his friend, although I joke with him he couldn't make me into a middle linebacker, no matter how hard he tried!

Getting us in the correct defense was my responsibility.

CHAPTER 21
CLOSING OUT MY CAREER AS A FOOTBALL PLAYER

Before the 1976 season, I made my decision that this this would be my 14th and final year in professional football. Having reached the age of 35, I really wanted to go out while I was still playing well and not a handicap to the team.

I know a lot of athletes don't want to admit that their day in the sun has come to an end, but I knew this was the right time for me to go out, and go out on my terms. At the same time, I was totally dedicated to helping the Cowboys have another championship season.

One of my old sidekicks at linebacker, Dave Edwards, had retired after the Super Bowl, leaving me as the senior member of the 1976 team. Mel Renfro, who had been a rookie in my second year, had the honor of being the second oldest Cowboy in 1975, and Mel was still playing at a high level as one of the best cornerbacks in the NFL.

The great Jethro Pugh, who had been a rookie in 1965, was still going strong, but it was an overall young football team that had all the promise of accomplishing what we had started a decade earlier.

Besides all those rookies who had performed so well in 1975, the Cowboys added a quality receiver in Butch Johnson and a big-time linebacker in Mike Hegman, who had been drafted with that 1975 bunch but still had a year to play in college.

After winning the first five games of the season, I think there was the feeling around the NFL that the Cowboys had all the ingredients to win the NFC East. But the Washington Redskins and St. Louis Cardinals were both still playing at an awfully high level, and we found out just how high when we played the Cardinals in Busch Stadium in our sixth game of the year.

St. Louis had a receiver named Mel Gray who caused us fits, catching two long touchdown passes from Jim Hart that offset a great day by Roger Staubach. We lost 21-17 and knew that once again the East would be a three-team race decided in the final few weeks of the season.

We were 6-1 when we traveled to Washington to play the Redskins, still coached by George Allen, where a young Joe Theismann was trying to unseat Billy Kilmer at quarterback. While the Redskins had a young, big and fast back in John Riggins, they also had a familiar face to Dallas fans, Calvin Hill.

Calvin, who had left us for the World Football League, was back in the NFL after the upstart WFL closed its doors for good a year earlier.

Our games against the Redskins in the 1970s were legendary, but this one was controlled completely by our defense. Only a last-minute touchdown pass from Theismann to Roy Jefferson kept it from being a shutout.

Regardless, we won 20-7, held the powerful Washington offense to less than 150 yards, sacked Kilmer and Theismann seven times and picked them off three more. There was little doubt after that convincing victory that we were the team to beat in the East.

Our inability to establish a running attack to set up our passing attack became more troublesome each week. After 9-3 and 17-10 wins over the New York Giants and Buffalo Bills, we lost a 17-10 game to Atlanta.

That should have been an omen of how those final weeks would go for us. There was one unforgettable trip down memory lane for me on Thanksgiving Day, 1976.

We hosted the Cardinals at Texas Stadium, and like so many of those previous Turkey Day games, this one was important because the winner would likely be the NFC East champion.

Like many of our Thanksgiving wins, Roger Staubach was the key, but this time he did more with his runs than his passing. He was our leading rusher that day and scored one of our touchdowns on a run and threw for the other on a short pass to fullback Scott Laidlaw.

A blocked punt for a safety by Hollywood Henderson gave us the cushion we needed to win 19-14. After that game, we needed only to win one of our final two to clinch the East.

We clinched our division in our next game, winning 26-7 at Philadelphia against an Eagle team that was going through a disappointing season. Roman Gabriel, whom I had battled against in college and in the pros when he was a Ram, was the Eagle quarterback. He was on the back half of his career and other than a brief moment when he flashed his old arm strength on a touchdown pass, Gabriel and the Eagles couldn't move the ball against us.

A touchdown pass from Roger to his new receiver Butch Johnson put the game out of reach, and the Cowboys were again champions of the East. It would mark the 10th time in my career that I would have the opportunity to compete in the playoffs, making me feel pretty proud about what we had achieved as a team.

Washington was our opponent in my final regular-season game in Dallas, and Billy Kilmer was back in control as the quarterback for the Redskins. While we knew our playoff position had been cinched a week earlier, Washington was battling our East rival St. Louis for the wildcard berth in the playoffs.

And Washington played like a team with everything on the line, while we lacked the intensity level to win the game. We trailed 10-7 at the half after Kilmer threw a short TD pass to Jean Fugett, a former teammate of mine in Dallas.

In the second half, Riggins really displayed his skills that would help him eventually be an All-Pro and Super Bowl MVP, but the clinching touchdown in the 27-14 Washington win came on a run by Calvin Hill.

Despite the loss to Washington, we entered the playoffs against the Los Angeles Rams, the same team we had beaten badly a year earlier on their home field. Having them home in Dallas and being a prohibitive favorite to beat them and meet either the Vikings or the Redskins for the NFC championship made us feel pretty good entering the 1976 playoffs.

Reflecting on the Los Angeles game, I guess the only good news was that it was the physical, knock-down, drag-out type of football that I enjoyed playing. The bad news was that we lost 14-12.

We had led 10-7 at the half, thanks to a blocked punt by Charlie Waters that set up a short TD run by Scott Laidaw.

It was still 10-7 in the fourth quarter until it appeared that the Rams had tied us at 10-10 after Tom Dempsey kicked a field goal. Rarely do you see a coach take points off the board, but Ram coach Chuck Knox did that afternoon.

It proved to be the right decision when Lawrence McCutcheon scored the go-ahead touchdown. After we failed to move the ball, we punted and the Rams were trying to run out the clock. But our defense hung tough and stopped them, forcing another punt right after the two-minute warning.

For the second time in the game, Charlie Waters blocked the punt and we recovered on the Ram 17-yard line. I doubt if anyone in Texas Stadium or those watching on TV thought we were going to lose.

On first down, Roger hit Butch Johnson for what we thought was a touchdown, but they ruled he didn't have both feet in bounds, negating the play. On fourth and two, Roger was tackled less than a yard short of a first down.

We still had some timeouts and used them while the Rams were taking a knee on the first three downs. On fourth down with the ball on the four-yard line Chuck Knoll made the right call. He told his punter Rusty Jackson to run out of the end zone and take a safety to make sure Charlie didn't have a chance to block a third punt. The final score was 14-12.

My career as a football player was over.

People have asked me if I got emotional in the locker room taking off my uniform for the final time. I was too numb from losing the game. I don't think anyone of us could believe what had happened.

I took off that jersey 55 for the final time and threw it into a pile with the others, knowing that I'd given it my all at Excel High School, and the University of Alabama and Dallas.

Heck, I was lucky enough to play on a national championship team for Coach Bryant and a Super Bowl championship team for Tom Landry. Although the NFL didn't officially start keeping defensive statistics until six years after I played my last game, the Cowboys' coaching staff had credited me with 743 primary tackles and assisting in 493 more.

Although my math isn't that good, I know that's 1,236 tackles. I'm proud that I started 154 consecutive games as a middle linebacker in the NFL, which I'm told is still the record for an inside backer.

I finished my career with 32 interceptions and ran three of those back for touchdowns. Only Miami Dolphin middle linebacker Nick Buoniconti had as many. I always felt I redeemed myself in the eyes of Gil Brandt, whose only reluctance in drafting me was the fact that I hadn't covered many passes while I was playing at Alabama.

There's no way that I can recount all the just magnificent players who I lined up with during those 14 years and my memories of them, or all the coaches either. Tom Landry is an NFL institution and rightfully so.

How many guys get to play 14 years for the same team with the same head coach and the same position coach? Jerry Tubbs, the man I replaced at

Coach Landry was my only head coach in the pros.

middle linebacker, coached me for 14 seasons. Talk about a great football man and better person, you can start with Jerry Tubbs.

He probably did more to teach me about being a professional than anyone, and he was a Cowboy institution as a player before I got to Dallas and long after as a coach until he retired from football in 1988.

From 1966 until I retired, the defensive coordinator for the "Doomsday Defense" was Ernie Stautner, who had been a tough old Marine in World War II before becoming a standout defensive lineman for the Steelers and Redskins in the NFL.

He helped make our defensive front tougher and helped push our defense to become one of legendary proportions.

Although Gene Stallings didn't come to Dallas until later on in my career, I can proudly say that I have the honor of being the only player who competed for him on the college and pro level, and although I had retired before the Dallas run to the 1977 championship, I'm glad that Coach Stallings had the chance to be part of a Super Bowl champion.

I left the NFL only regretting that I hadn't done more to help my teammates win some of those games we lost on the road to the Super Bowl, but there's no way to tell you how proud I was to make it there. Not only that, but to have been chosen captain to represent all those great Cowboy players is a legacy that I'm most proud.

As I made my way home to Biddie and our three sons at the end of 1976, I did it with the determination that I would succeed in whatever path God lead me. And I really didn't have a clear cut idea of where the road might lead.

TIME OUT: D.D. LEWIS

D.D. Lewis was an All-American at Mississippi State in 1966 before joining the Dallas Cowboys. He would become a mainstay at linebacker alongside Lee Roy and become a close friend as well.

We had something rare and special during our years with the Cowboys.

It was a bond that you usually see on high school teams or college teams. The entertainment business has now become such a big part of it, along with free agency. When Lee Roy and I played, you stayed with the same team and you developed lifelong friendships.

I was a rookie in 1967, being drafted in the fifth round. John Douglas from Missouri and Ed Harmon from Louisville were drafted ahead of me.

I had played some center at Mississippi State, back in the last days when players went both ways. Dallas needed a center, but the Cowboys also needed help at outside linebacker and I ended up playing my whole career on the outside.

One day I had a good practice and Lee Roy came up to me in the cafeteria and said that I'd done well. Rookies usually didn't get much praise from the veterans. It was such a revolving door in the pros during the pre-season that a lot of rookies weren't around long enough to even know the veterans.

My first impression of Lee Roy was this bowlegged guy from Alabama wasn't all that big, but he had big strong hands and a washboard stomach. On the field, he was the fiercest competitor I'd ever seen. He gave 100 percent not only in the games but in practice. I know it had an impact on me, and I know it had an impact on every player trying to make the team.

When you make the team, you start recognizing people and watching their habits. And the player I emulated was Lee Roy Jordan. My second year with Dallas, I remember losing to Cleveland in the playoffs.

After the game, Lee Roy and Biddie, along with Dave Edwards and Bob Lilly, asked me to join them for what we thought was going to be a post-game celebration. Those guys knew how to build bonds off the field and make you feel a part of the team.

The only thing I'm sorry for Lee Roy is that he didn't become a coach. He wouldn't have put up with any nonsense from his players, but he would have pushed them to the limit to be champions in all phases of their lives. I can assure you that he would have taught fundamentals and techniques like few coaches could have.

He was a coach on the field, a leader like few others. He was an absolute master at calling plays. He knew what every player was supposed to do on each play, and he knew all of the strengths and weaknesses of an opposing offense.

Coach Landry wouldn't give the backup players a game plan, because the starters never left the game unless there was an injury. To say the least, it's very difficult to stay attentive and involved when you knew you weren't going to play. But Lee Roy was always there, making sure we knew what we were supposed to do if we did play.

In 1971, we started out 3-4 and were a floundering team. Lee Roy got the team together and told us he expected everyone in the room to be committed to winning the rest of our games, and if anyone wasn't committed, then he needed to be gone. We won the rest of our games and the Super Bowl. That was Lee Roy being the leader.

He taught me a lot about playing and practicing enthusiastically. He taught me about being a leader. He taught me about being accessible and being a Dallas Cowboy and sacrificing for the community.

Every year there was a golf tournament in Dallas at his club, and he'd be out there hustling golf bags for the pros, helping them feel welcome to the city. A lot of them didn't know who he was, and he didn't tell them. They probably thought he was a local yokel, when in reality he was one of the biggest names in Dallas, a bigger name than any of them. That's the type of man he is.

I'll never forget the year after he retired, we were going through a tough practice on a hot day in Dallas. There was a fence around the practice field, and I had taken a knee, catching my breath. This guy had climbed to the top of the fence and yelled, "Hey, get off your blanking knee and get out there and play football."

It was Lee Roy. Of course, he could have just walked into practice, but that was Lee Roy. He was just a fan then, but a vocal one!

I still go hunting with Lee Roy every year. If he doesn't kill anything, he'll walk you to death. And, we'll talk about the Mississippi State-Alabama game that year. Most of the time he'll get the last laugh on that one.

I feel unbelievably lucky to have played for the Dallas Cowboys for 13 seasons and having had the opportunity to play alongside Lee Roy.

Here I am late in my career as a Cowboy.

CHAPTER 22
LIFE AFTER FOOTBALL

When I retired from the Dallas Cowboys, I was 35 years old and had Biddie and my three sons David, Lee and Chris to look after. We sure didn't make enough money playing in the NFL back then to retire, so I started looking for a new job.

I was frankly relieved to be retired from football. After playing 14 years in the NFL, four at Alabama, and five in high school, it was enough. That takes a lot of toll on the body, and I felt pretty lucky to have to come out of it in relatively good physical shape.

Nevertheless, I knew I was going to miss the game, and I was nervous about just what the next years would hold for me and my family.

Naturally, I thought about going into coaching, feeling that football had been my life and I could teach young players how to play the game fundamentally in the correct manner and with a winning attitude. I had been a student of the game, and had learned all aspects about football, not only on defense but on offense and the kicking game.

I visited with Coach Landry about staying on with the Cowboys, but he was honest, telling me that assistant coaches just didn't make that much money. He thought I'd have success going into business. I think Coach Landry was paying his assistants in the $30,000 range.

I also set up a meeting with Coach Bryant in Tuscaloosa to talk to him about helping me get into coaching. That was in early 1977, and he was even more honest about the fact that coaches just didn't make any money. He was making $35,000 a year as head coach and athletic director, and he was paying his two coordinators – Mal Moore and Ken Donahue – $22,000 a year.

Over the years, that certainly changed. But that's just the way it was in those days, so I put on a coat and tie and set out to find a new career.

When I played for the Cowboys, just about every player had an off-season job, preparing for the future as well as making a little money. I worked in the real estate business, primarily developing large warehouses. I learned about making a profit, keeping books, and how to run a company. The experience was invaluable.

I also worked in real estate brokerage and became friends with Claude McClennahan. He really taught me the commercial real estate business, especially developing lands for offices and malls. I saw firsthand how people invested in the commercial real estate market and made money doing it.

Another great businessman in Dallas who was a friend and teacher was Bobby Folsom. Bobby served as mayor of Dallas from 1975-81, and he's just a straight shooter and honest as a day is long. He made quite a bit of money in commercial real estate and taught me about keeping detailed records and making sure I always covered my expenses.

He's just a lifelong friend as well as a great mentor. He encouraged me to go into business and apply all the lessons I had learned on the football field as well as what I had learned in my off-season positions.

I really thought that I would end up owning and running an automobile dealership, but a deal to purchase one fell through. I wasn't discouraged, which is certainly a lesson I learned all too well playing football.

A banker friend of mine told that there was a terrific man in the lumber business who was getting older and was looking to slow down. I'm unemployed, so I'm willing to meet with anyone, so I went to meet Kenneth Moore.

I can't begin to tell you the unbelievable relationship we developed over a lunch that went on and on. Within three months, I was the owner of two lumber businesses, one in Dallas and the other in Austin.

Mr. Moore financed a lot of it himself and told me I could pay him off in 20 years. That's what I did. I never missed a payment.

Many years later, I got a call from one of the lumber companies in California that I'd been doing business with for 20 years, and they told me Kenneth Moore had signed a letter of credit that said he would pay bills if I couldn't. He guaranteed it, and I didn't even know it. I didn't even know they needed any extra collateral.

It was an unbelievable gesture on his part. Mr. Moore and I had a father-son relationship, and his commitment and desire to see me succeed is something that I can't really repay. He was just a terrific gentleman.

I think he took a lot of pride that I took over the business he had started and made it grow. I think he also took a lot of pride that I never had to lean on him for any financial assistance.

Lee Roy Jordan Lumber Company specializes in bringing in redwood from California and cedar from Canada. Mr. Moore gave me the motivation and understanding about how to develop the company. I'm proud to say that our annual sales are now $43 million. And it's a pretty good-sized company.

My oldest son David has been in the business since he graduated from Washington and Lee University, and he does most of the work these days. Actually, I had encouraged him to find something else, because I didn't know if it was a good idea for him to be in business with me.

I set up a luncheon with Bob Folsom, knowing that he would give David some sound advice. One of the first things he said was, "David, if you can go into your family's business, do it. It will be the best thing you will ever do."

I guess that showed how much I knew!

David is now the president of our company and has done a super job of making it grow. My youngest son Chris is another key member of our operation. We have terrific employees, people who perform extremely well in every assignment they are given.

Chris oversees all of our facilities, vehicles and equipment, which believe me is a major undertaking. Our middle son Lee runs a general valve company in Saraland, Alabama.

Actually, it's a company that I started years ago with my brother, but sold it. Lee is the general manager and they have some pretty important clients, including Alabama Power.

I have one manager of Lee Roy Jordan Lumber, Ray Morgan, who came to work for me as a yard guy when he was still in high school. He's been a great employee, and today, he is my facility manager just south of Dallas at our wholesale division and has done a terrific job.

We have changed locations a couple of times. We moved our Austin business to Houston, and later we moved to Hillsborough, Texas, to reduce transporting costs. We do a lot of business in Oklahoma, Kansas, Alabama, Tennessee and Louisiana as well as Texas, so having the two facilities close to one another just makes the best business sense.

We do a lot of siding for houses and apartments as well as redwood for decks and patios. One of our biggest products now are exposed beams in restaurants, golf courses, clubhouses and office buildings. Douglas firs are also a big seller for us, and they are used in the beams.

I also owned a ranch in east Texas after I retired from football, but I sold it when my kids were out of school. When the boys were growing up, I'd make them go out there and learn how to work cattle and horses. I think it was a great experience for each of my sons.

There was one really sad moment for me during those years, and that was January 26, 1983. Coach Bryant always kept in touch with his former players, and I like to think that I had a special bond with a special man.

Throughout the 1982 football season, I would call his secretary, Linda Knowles, to check on him, because it was painfully apparent that his health was failing. That was hard for me to accept because he had always presented such an imposing presence. Linda told me that he wasn't doing well and how concerned she was about him.

I wasn't surprised when he announced his retirement in the middle of December, but when I got the call on January 26, telling me Coach Bryant had passed away, it was still a shock. I headed to Tuscaloosa to be there with my former teammates and Coach Bryant's family.

I don't think any man in football has ever had, or will have, so many legendary figures of the game attend his funeral and burial. They came from all corners of the country to say their goodbyes. He was a man whom I'm not sure anyone has ever adequately described.

Most of us who went to play for him and stayed for four years became men. I like to think that I join the long list of those who had success in life and learned his lessons that sacrifice for the team leads to special moments in your life.

He had that quote, "If you have dedication and pride, and never quit, you'll be a winner. The price of victory is high, but so are the rewards." And, he was so right.

I still have his list of how to build a team on my office wall and I read it every day I'm there. There was only one Paul Bryant, and I'm lucky to have had him help me in my life.

Through the years, I told every coach, athletic director and president at the university, if they ever needed my help, just to call, and I'll be there.

In 1999, I was asked to serve on the selection commitee for the athletic director's position. When I heard that Dr. Andrew Sorensen was rumored to be talking to candidates that were not on the committee's list, I did call him and tell him that if it were true, I didn't want to be part of the selection committee.

Ultimately, our recommendation of Mal Moore was accepted, and I think the job Mal did speaks for itself. It's not an easy job, but Alabama needed someone who understood that the fans were splintered and money had to be raised to rebuild facilities that had fallen into disrepair.

Mal's hiring of Nick Saban will always be looked upon as his finest hour as director. However, if he hadn't had the foresight to go out and raise money and build top-level football facilities, Nick Saban would have never come to Tuscaloosa.

I think I'm like all the former players who are just thankful for the job Nick has done as the head coach in returning the Crimson Tide to the elite status of college football. You know when his teams take the field that they will be trained at their highest level to win, and if they don't, it won't be because they weren't well coached.

Faith, family and football have always been the most important aspects of my life. As I said at the start, the church has always been an integral part of the lives of the Jordan Family. I believe in the Bible and feel blessed to have had a large and loving family.

Biddie and I have our three sons and three wonderful daughters-in-law, Melanie, Lisa and Nikki. Our eight grandchildren are really a blessing to our family. Our two oldest granddaughters, Julia and Mary Beth, Lee's children, are at the University of Alabama now, and that makes me proud.

Our other grandchildren are Kathryn, Bradford, Meredith, Dabney, Thomas and Bryant, and they are all very special to us.

I have always gone to the Catholic church with Biddie. I always felt that a relationship an individual has with God is a special one, no matter what church a person belongs to. For 49 years, I had gone to church with her, but sometimes I had also gone to my church as well.

In 2012, I met a priest in Dallas, and I just loved his message and his energy. Monsignor Milam Joseph really inspired me with his enthusiasm and his commitment to Christ.

Biddie was out of town for a few days on a girls' trip. It's an annual trip that some of the wives of former Cowboy players have been going on for 36 years.

I went to Monsignor Joseph and asked him if I could become a member of the Catholic church. He was delighted that I wanted to join the church, and he knew I'd been going to the Catholic church with Biddie for nearly 50 years.

When she got back, I told Biddie what I had done. Oh, my gosh, she was so happy and pleased, and told me that it was one of the best things I'd ever done for her. It was a special moment in our lives.

I've been lucky enough to have had five coaches that I wouldn't trade for anything, the first being my father Walter. He taught me the principles that have sustained me throughout my life, including being honest with people in all my dealings. I lost my dad a few months before Coach Bryant passed away.

My mother Cleo was a head coach in her own right and reinforced everything I learned from my father. She instilled in me the concept of always trying to help other people. She passed away three years after my dad.

I'm proud that our lifelong family friend and childhood minister Carey Robertson returned to Excel to officiate their respective funerals. He's ministered all over the world and for him to take time to come back to the early roots of his ministry, I think, says a lot about the love he had for my folks.

My high school coach, W.C. Majors, gave me a start in football and taught me how to play the game and be a good teammate. He was a legendary high school coach in Alabama, and a man I always went to see when I came back home.

Coach Bryant and Coach Landry epitomized the truth of a real competitor. You win with dignity and lose with class. They usually won, but when they didn't, they would accept the blame for the shortcomings. That takes a special man to do that.

I didn't know it at the time but Coaches Bryant and Landry shared the same birthday, September 11. Coach Landry died in 2000 and he left a legacy in the NFL that made him a legend.

Some former players say they regret playing football. Not me. I've had seven operations, new knees, new shoulders and a new hip; but that doesn't take away from the fun I had playing.

Football served as an avenue for me to meet presidents of the United States and CEOs of major corporations. Football enabled meet to even meet my childhood heroes, Elvis and John Wayne! Football helped me to understand all the concepts of teamwork and sacrifice for the good of the team for the goal of being a champion.

Football allowed me to be a champion at Alabama and Dallas. Football allowed me to be a captain on two of the most well-known football programs in the sport. I'd like to think I'd have been successful if not for the game of football, but I wouldn't trade being a player for the Excel Panthers, Alabama Crimson Tide or Dallas Cowboys for anything.

HAPPY DAYS BACK IN ALABAMA

Biddie and I have spent the past 20 years dividing our time between Dallas and Point Clear, Alabama. Our home is on Mobile Bay and we like to spend at least six months there.

We call our home "Fourth Quarter" because one day we realized that we were in the fourth quarter of our lives, and the best gift we could give our children and grandkids is memories of fun times during our summers in Alabama on Mobile Bay.

Our son Lee, his wife Lisa and their three daughters live nearby and that makes being there even more enjoyable.

We have many dear friends in Point Clear, including some college friends from our days at the University of Alabama. We have made quite a few new friends as well. Our way of life is peaceful, quite the contrast from the high energy and demands of Dallas. While we do not intend to give up our life and friends in Dallas, it sure is nice to share the best of both places.

I have a golf group that I especially enjoy in Point Clear. Joe Bullard, Clifton Inge, Win Thurber, Kenny McLean, Mason McGowin and Champ Meyercord make up our usual group. While we have many fun days playing golf and sharing stories, they always love getting my money when my game is not at its best.

Biddie has wonderful group of girlfriends. She started a canasta group a few years ago, and they just might have more fun than our golf group.

During football season, we try to attend as many Alabama games as possible. We even have a hunting cabin on family land just 30 minutes from Tuscaloosa. With two granddaughters attending the University of Alabama, it is a fun gathering place during the football season as well as holidays and hunting season. We were born in Alabama and even after living in Dallas for more than 50 years – Alabama is still home!

When I was growing up in Mobile, the first two things I learned from my father were the Lord's Prayer and the Tulane Fight Song. In high school, I played football at UMS-Wright and was invited to Tulane on an official visit.

The player that Tulane really wanted was Jimmy Dill, who was the best player in the Mobile area. The Tulane coaches spent most of the time recruiting Jimmy, and I guess I was disappointed. Jimmy ended up signing with Alabama, and I decided to go to school there. It was the best decision I ever made in my life.

One of Jimmy's suitemates was a player from Excel, Alabama, Lee Roy Jordan. I was visiting Jimmy one day and met Lee Roy for the first time. We had an immediate connection and became not only friends, but lifelong friends.

We both liked cattle and I guess we talked more about raising cattle, particularly Black Angus more than anything, including football. We were walking down the hall of the dormitory, and it was easy to see the respect the other players had for Lee Roy. He was not only the best player around, but he was their leader.

Coach (Paul) Bryant wanted his players to concentrate on football all the time, so I guess Lee Roy probably got some relief talking to me about cattle! His wife Biddie likes to tell the story about walking across campus, holding Lee Roy's hand. When they saw Coach Bryant walking toward them, she said that Lee Roy almost threw her in the shrubbery to keep Coach Bryant from seeing him with his girlfriend!

Lee Roy said Coach Bryant feared girlfriends could be a distraction and he didn't want a coed messing up the team.

Obviously, I saw Lee Roy play a lot of games, but the one I remember most in his college days was the Senior Bowl in Mobile. That's the day he got his teeth knocked out, but he just kept on playing and led a goal-line stand at the end of the game to win it for the South team.

One area where Lee Roy didn't have a lot of luck was with that new car he got when he signed with the Dallas Cowboys. Gil Brandt signed him and got him a Buick Riviera as his signing bonus. I met Gil at a function in Dallas and he told me the story about driving the car to Tuscaloosa but hitting a cow in Mississippi and wrecking it.

When he finally got the Riviera fixed, Lee Roy and I were driving to a cattle sale somewhere outside of Tuscaloosa. We passed a car and this guy threw a beer can out and hit Lee Roy's new car. Those guys jumped out of the car. They were mad but all I can say is Lee Roy gave them an attitude adjustment. They then gave him a couple of hundred dollars to fix the dent in the Riviera.

After Lee Roy started his career in Dallas, I opened an office in Long Beach, Calif. The Cowboys had their training camp in Thousand Oaks and I'd see him during training camp with the Cowboys. When they had a night off, he'd come down to Long Beach., and I got to meet a lot of the Dallas players during that time.

Years later, Lee Roy received the ultimate honor for a Cowboy, induction into the Ring of Honor. I have to admit it's one of the most humbling moments for me as well. Lee Roy was allowed to have one guest attend with him, and he invited me to come up from Mobile.

I have a signed picture from that day of Lee Roy and all the other inductees. I'm talking about players like Bob Lilly, Roger Staubach, Don Meredith, Jethro Pugh. True football legends.

During one of the functions that weekend, I was visiting with Jethro. He was a super, nice man. He told me that Lee Roy was the catalyst for the great Doomsday Defense. He said when Lee Roy was out of the game, all the other players on defense would look to the sideline and want to know when he was coming back in the game.

He went on to tell me that he always knew when the other team was running his way, because Lee Roy would signal to let him know. I guess that's why when Lee Roy was out of the game, his teammates wanted him back out there as soon as possible.

When I mentioned Gil Brandt earlier, I should have mentioned that he told me that he built the entire Dallas defense around Lee Roy. Gil also said he was glad he had drafted him before the 1962 Orange Bowl when Lee Roy put on a show, making 31 unassisted tackles. Obviously, meaning some other team may have picked him before Dallas got its pick in the first round.

Every year around the time of the legendary Ice Bowl game in Green Bay, they'll show highlights and I'll call Lee Roy and tell him, "You went the wrong way again on the quarterback sneak by Bart Starr." He'll mumble something back, but that's all in fun, you know.

Every time we talk on the phone, Lee Roy tells me he loves me before he hangs up. We will quote Bible verses to each other as well, and I just always feel better after talking to him.

He's a unique man, far more than just a man who happened to be a great football player.

When I arrived at the University of Alabama as a young assistant coach in 1958, it was no secret that Auburn was pretty much dominating the state, having won the national championship the previous season.

We needed football players. And, we wanted young men who excelled in all facets of their lives, because we knew we had to have those type of individuals with the right makeup, mentally and physically, to return the Crimson Tide to its rightful spot in the college football hierarchy.

My old teammate at Texas A&M, Bobby Drake Keith, was the coach who found a player in Excel, Alabama, who fit everything we thought we needed to be successful. His name was Lee Roy Jordan.

I don't think there were but a handful of people outside his hometown who had ever heard of Lee Roy in the fall of 1958, but by the time he finished his career in Dallas, everybody who knew anything about football knew his name.

Lee Roy was the perfect player for Coach (Paul) Bryant because he embodied all the principles that Coach tried to instill in all of us who were fortunate enough to have played or coached for him.

There was never a practice or a game that Lee Roy didn't give 100 percent effort. There was never a time he backed down from a challenge. There was never a time that he put himself ahead of the team and its goals. Man, that's a coach's dream.

Just think about that and put it into perspective. So many great players are more concerned about their own achievements than the good of the team. Lee Roy Jordan wanted his team to be champions first and foremost.

In 1961, we knew we had the makings of a championship team at Alabama, because it meant so much to all the players, but especially to Lee Roy. Coach Bryant once said, "That team played like it was a sin to give up a point."

And that's exactly how they played. We only gave up 25 points the entire season, and I promise you the opposing teams were lucky to get those few points. They had to earn each one.

I know that's how Lee Roy approached every game. There was the time when we were playing Auburn and had a big lead in the fourth quarter, but they were threatening near our goal line. Lee Roy put himself into the game to make sure they didn't. In his four years at Alabama, Auburn never scored a point on us.

Naturally, I followed his career with the Dallas Cowboys, where he became an All-Pro and the leader of one of the NFL's best defensive teams. In 1972, Coach Tom Landry offered me the opportunity to join the Dallas staff and a second chance to be teamed with Lee Roy.

Every coach, every player, and every worker for the Cowboys knew Lee Roy Jordan was the leader of the Cowboy defense. Just think about this: Lee Roy had been captain of the 1962 Alabama team.

Early in his career at Dallas, he was named the defensive captain. There aren't many players who were so respected that they became captains for two of the most legendary coaches in the history of football, Paul Bryant and Tom Landry.

Being a captain may be the ultimate testament to a player's leadership abilities, and Lee Roy had tons of that. More importantly, his teammates respected him. If there was a problem on the team, you could bet Lee Roy was going to step up and do his best to fix it.

On the field, his records speak volumes. He has the most consecutive starts ever by a middle linebacker. He has the most interceptions by a middle linebacker. He led us in tacking every year. He called the defenses for Dallas for 13 straight years. Some players hurry off to the locker room as soon as practice is over. Not Lee Roy.

Jerry Tubbs was the linebacker coach but he didn't have a strong throwing arm. So, Lee Roy asked me to stay after practice, to work on his footwork in dropping back in pass coverage.

I'd play quarterback and throw him a zillion passes so he could improve his hands, helping him make those interceptions. Here's a man who was already as good a middle linebacker as you'd ever want to have, but he was never complacent. He always wanted to improve.

Anybody who saw Lee Roy play knows how good a player he was, but he's an even better man. How many people can look back on their lives and say, "I was good at my job but I was a better husband, a better father, a better friend?"

Well Lee Roy has been all that and more.

That's who Lee Roy really is. Football provided him with an avenue to achieve his dreams, but I have no doubt he would have been a winner and a success no matter what profession he chose.

I feel lucky and honored that he decided to play for the University of Alabama, and then honored to reunite with him in Dallas. I am thankful he asked me to say a few words about him.

I feel even luckier that my family has been friends with Lee Roy and Biddie for all these years. They are grade-A people.

When I reflect back on my own career in athletics, I feel humbled to have been affiliated with true giants of the game of football. And, let me assure Lee Roy Jordan is right there with the best of them.

Anyone who loves the Crimson Tide or the Cowboys or just the game of football, should take time to read these pages about a legend of the game, my old player and friend Lee Roy Jordan.

LEE ROY JORDAN HONORS

– All-SEC Sophomore Team, 1960

– Bluebonnet Bowl Defensive MVP, 1960

– 2nd-team All-American, 1961

– All-SEC, 1961

– Consensus All-American, 1962

– Team Captain, 1962

– SEC Defensive Player of Year, 1962

– Alabama -record 31 tackles vs. Oklahoma, 1963

– Orange Bowl Defensive MVP, 1963

– 1st-Round Draft Pick, Dallas Cowboys, 1963

– Senior Bowl, 1963

– College All-Star Game, 1963

– SEC Team of the Decade for 1960s

– SEC Defensive Player of the Decade for 1960s

– Alabama Player of the Decade for 1960s

– NFL All-Pro, 1969, 1973

– Dallas record 21 tackles vs. Philadelphia, 1971

– Team Captain, Super Bowl VI Champions, 1972

– Cover of Sports Illustrated 1973

– NFL Defensive Player of the Year, 1973

LEE ROY JORDAN HONORS

– NFL Pro Bowl, 1967-68-69-73-74

– NFC Defensive Player of the Year, 1973

– NFL-Record 3 Interceptions in a quarter, 1973

– Most Consecutive Starts by a Middle Linebacker (154), 1965-76

– Tied for Most Career Interceptions by a Middle Linebacker (32)

– State of Alabama Sports Hall of Fame, 1980

– All-Time SEC Team, 1983

– College Football Hall of Fame, 1983

– Orange Bowl Hall of Fame, 1984

– Senior Bowl Hall of Fame, 1988

– Dallas Cowboy Silver Anniversary All-Time Team, 1984

– Dallas Cowboy Ring of Honor, 1989

– ESPN's All-Time College Football Team, 1991

– All-Time Alabama Centennial Team, 1992

– 3 Interceptions in a quarter vs. Cincinnati picked as one of
10 best moments in Texas Stadium, 2008

– State of Texas Hall of Fame, 2008

– Football Writers All-Time College Team, 2015

SPECIAL THANKS

I want to thank the following people who were so helpful in helping make this project happen. Kim Bryan, who assisted Steve Townsend, in interviewing my former teammates, edited this book. Sadly, Kim's husband Courtney Haden passed away earlier this year after a short illness. Courtney had spent numerous hours recording all the interviews with me as well as the others who graciously talked about playing with me. Without Kim's and Courtney's help, we would have never gotten the book published.

Also, Paul Bryant Junior and Paul Camp were kind enough to read the book to make sure I hadn't made many mistakes. Ken Gaddy and Brad Green of the Bryant Museum went out of their way to help as well. Brent Hollingsworth helped with the design and layout of the book and cover.

Finally, thanks to each one of you who takes time to read my story. I hope you find it as interesting as I did reflecting on my days in Excel, Tuscaloosa and Dallas.

Kindest Regards,

Lee Roy Jordan

Lee Roy Jordan